TYPES OF

GETTING TO KNOW THE

BIRDS

IN YOUR NEIGHBOURHOOD

Rainbow Lorikeet
in flight, revealing
its amazing colours
and markings

GETTING TO KNOW THE
BIRDS
IN YOUR NEIGHBOURHOOD

A FIELD GUIDE

DARRYL JONES

NEWSOUTH

CONTENTS

White-faced Heron
on the hunt

Part 3 🐦 Next level bird watching

Male Scarlet Honeyeater
with callistemon pollen
on its head

INTRODUCTION

In recent years, we've seen an extraordinary growth in interest in and appreciation of the wildlife that lives around us, in our yards, local parks and nearby bushland. This has been an unexpected outcome – a rare positive – of the global COVID pandemic. Being forced to stay near home and limited to our backyards or local parks, many of us noticed – often for the first time – the variety and abundance of birds living nearby.

Birds are often noisy, colourful and moving, so they draw our attention. They are also active during the day; most of Australia's mammals are nocturnal, and reptiles and frogs tend to hide well away from human eyes.

Stuck at home, we became aware of the birds visiting our backyards, hunting for insects among the shrubs, sipping nectar from the grevilleas or perhaps making use of a bird feeder or two. Of course, the birds had always been there; we'd just been too busy to see them.

Where birds had simply been part of the background – just a component of the suburban soundtrack, perhaps a pleasant splash of colour, but not much more – having the time to stop and look at them properly made a big difference. It was as though we actually 'saw' them for the first time. Even familiar, commonplace species seen up close are surprisingly beautiful. But more than their looks, many of these birds began to stand out as individuals with distinctive personalities, living their lives alongside ours. Carrying on as though we were part of *their* background.

For a lot of people, these seemingly simple encounters with local birds resulted in a genuine change in perspective. The birds were appreciated for their colourful and exuberant presence at a time of widespread uncertainty. They offered proof that not everything was doom and gloom; nature was resilient and continued on despite our woes and anxieties. The birds were living their lives with all their usual energy and purpose. Perhaps we could glean a lesson in there somewhere ...

This book aims to help you to really get to know the birds that live in your neighbourhood. Your backyard, the park across the street, the bushland reserve on the other side of your suburb. It might even help you feel better about yourself and your life. That's a serious claim by the way: watching birds is proven to enhance mental wellbeing and help recovery from depression (see *Can bird watching make you happy?*, p. 204).

There are, however, some requirements for anyone interested in becoming a bird watcher. The main two are obtaining some binoculars (we will discuss this later) and working out how to identify the birds you are looking at. A lot of people approach the ID problem the same way they try to solve most of the other queries in their lives: Google it! But how do you do that? What question would you ask to get a sensible answer? Artificial Intelligence is undoubtedly going to help one day, but we're not there yet.

What about taking a picture and asking the algorithm to match it? Despite the extraordinary capacities of many smart phone cameras, most are not quite good enough to zoom in close enough, just yet. But even a fuzzy picture may be useful if you want to try and match it yourself. And a number of Apps can assist; some even use the bird's calls as the key way to identify the bird (see *References and useful resources*, p. 211). All these technological tools can be useful and should be explored. But none is foolproof. Nor can they guarantee correct identification. That will – and should – take time to develop.

We think that you should try to get to know your local birds, not just give them a name and move on. Unashamedly, we think that bird watching should be captivating. Enthralling. Definitely entertaining, as engrossing as any Netflix blockbuster. The birds that live around us are living out their complicated, fascinating lives, right in front of us. Discovering and learning from them by careful, respectful observing can literally open up your world.

Our first bird watchers

Before we dive in and meet some of the birds that live around us, it's important to acknowledge the wisdom and relationships the First Nations peoples who live on this continent have with these creatures. They have an extremely sophisticated understanding of Australia's biodiversity, and the ways in which they interact with birds – and all wildlife – are complex and profound.

You don't develop these kinds of relationships without deep understanding and learning, forged over millennia. And a good way to illustrate this is to consider how many Indigenous names some species have. Take the familiar Willie Wagtail, for example, a bird found everywhere on the continent. This bird is associated with at least 66 names by First Nations naturalists, the most of any species, and that number is only those recorded by early European explorers and anthropologists. Although officially this bird is the Willie Wagtail, *Rhipidura leucophrys*, it is known on Country as cherrup cherrup, duwendira, deereeree, dhirriirrii, dhirridhirri, djitidjiti, jindirr-jindirr/jigir-jigir, jigirrjigirr, jitta jitta, jenning-gherrie, mugana, picata, tityarokan, thirri-tyirri, tjerrap tjerrap, wellpillup and wilaring (as well as lots of other names we are not permitted to use). This is hardly surprising; this small flycatcher is one of the most frequently mentioned species in First Nations stories from around the continent. As the people on Cape York advise, we should all 'listen carefully to what it has to say'.

Listen carefully? This seems good advice when it comes to our first bird watchers, too. Thankfully, there are many generous First Nations naturalists willing to share some of their knowledge and wisdom. You'll get a glimpse of that in the following pages, but there is far more to be learned beyond this little book. And if you are willing to listen, you will discover a lot more than how to tell the difference between species of egrets or lorikeets.

BIRD
WATCHING
101

Noisy Miners plotting
something nasty

WHY DO WE NEED THIS BOOK?

I REMEMBER THE MOMENT ALL TOO CLEARLY. I WAS IN MY EARLY TEENS AND HAD JUST PURCHASED MY FIRST BIRD IDENTIFICATION BOOK AND WAS KEEN TO GIVE IT A TEST RUN.

Although I had been interested in birds for years, and was becoming pretty good at finding them and observing their activities, I really wasn't at all certain which species I was looking at. Lots of the local birds had popular names, but I knew they weren't their 'real' names. Being able to identify a bird and give it its proper, accepted name – with confidence – is really important, especially if it might be a species you haven't seen before. Now that I had a decent guide book, everything was going to be different.

The bird I had spotted was not particularly exciting, but it seemed different to rather similar-looking species that were common in the area. I thought it was probably a honeyeater – a group of birds I felt I knew reasonably well. These abundant, spirited little sprites are typically found in the foliage of gum trees, flitting about in perpetual motion, gleaning insects and having minor disputes with their mates. The most prominent honeyeaters around central New South Wales where I lived were known as 'Greenies'. Their real name is White-plumed Honeyeater, although I didn't know that at the time. But the new bird looked slightly different from the image I still had in my mind.

This was the first bird I tried to identify in my shiny new field guide. I found the section on honeyeaters in the index and turned to the appropriate page. Actually, pages! Many pages of seemingly endless pictures of what seemed to be almost identical species. There must have been almost 20 other small greenish honeyeaters with very little in the way of distinctive features. My initial elation quickly evaporated. Instead of my new guidebook filling me with confidence at my identification skills, I felt exactly the opposite. How on earth would I be able to tell all these species apart, especially when they are difficult to observe for more than a few seconds?

Female Olive-backed Sunbird feeding a spider to its chick

And it wasn't just the honeyeaters. Similar frustrations occurred when I tried to distinguish between the species in other groups such as thornbills, cuckoos, quails and all those brownish fairy-wrens. And don't get me started on waders!

It wasn't clear to me at the time, but I came to realise that one of the main reasons for my bewilderment was that the guidebooks included all the species ever seen in the entire country. And Australia is a gigantic continent, with rainforests, deserts, woodlands, wetlands and (briefly) snow-capped mountains. There are also lots of islands, from the steamy tropics to the frigid Southern Ocean. A field guide of the birds occurring in the entire country with all those places and habitats has to include the lot: over 900 species!

This means that those honeyeater pages included species found in Far North Queensland, the vast central deserts and the islands of Bass Strait. No wonder there were so many. The reality was: only a handful of all those very similar honeyeaters actually occurred in my little patch of the continent. Eventually, I learned that most of the birds depicted could be ignored by referring to the little map showing where they were found. I could then concentrate on a much smaller group that occurred locally. (My new species was a Fuscous Honeyeater, by the way.)

Such frustrations are common, I know, among lots of people when they first begin to take their casual bird watching a bit more seriously. The major steps of purchasing a decent pair of binoculars and a bird field guide are often followed by feeling inadequate and out of your depth.

The sheer numbers of similar-looking species, and sometimes the terminology used to describe them, can cause genuine confusion. Instead of feeling excited and pleased about making an identification, plenty of beginners feel uncertain and far from confident. Too often the binoculars go unused and the guidebook is left unopened.

This book attempts to avoid that frustration. Its primary aims are to help make watching birds more interesting and to make identifying them as easy as possible. Instead of wanting to give up, you should feel encouraged to learn more, and have plenty of fun along the way. Right now, a lot of people are watching birds for the first time, and we want to encourage and enrich that experience.

While enabling you to identify the birds that live nearby is important, we also hope that finding out their names is just the start. One of the best things about bird watching – anywhere – is the very real possibility of something completely unexpected turning up. Even in the most familiar spots, where you think you know every species, a migrating cuckoo or storm-blown seabird may appear out of nowhere.

I recall vividly the day an exhausted Red-tailed Tropicbird landed in a carpark in Armidale in northern New South Wales, a very long way from the sea. A particularly large cyclone had pushed many seabirds inland, far from their normal routes. The arrival of a spectacular tropical island bird in a country town was bewildering for both the bird and the local bird watchers. You never know what you might see tomorrow; that's just one of the reasons to keep looking.

The next New Thing is always attractive but can also be a fleeting pleasure or superficial experience. What we hope to do with this book is enable you to see even familiar species as worth getting to know more closely. To go beyond simply making a list and moving on to the next bird, allowing yourself the time to watch and observe them closely. To be curious. Why are the Noisy Miners always chasing other species away? What are all those cockatoos doing out there on the football field? And why are the Rainbow Lorikeets eating the meat put out for the Magpies?

One of the key skills we hope you will develop is carefully observing the birds we share our cities with. This will take some practice and plenty of patience but is definitely worthwhile. There are several traditional elements to becoming a good naturalist: slow down, watch closely, take notes, ask questions and share with others. We would add another: enjoy. It can be a life-affirming, heart-filling, wonder-appreciating experience.

That may seem a bit fuzzy for the modern scientific ecologist. Surely, we need a serious, pragmatic approach to this pastime? After all, gathering information is critically important, especially as we face a multitude of global catastrophes including the climate crisis and the shocking decline in biodiversity. Many of you will be concerned and confronted by these immense problems.

Solving them requires collecting and making sense of as much reliable information – data – as possible. There are many ways that anyone, even complete beginners, can contribute to this important mission. Numerous 'Citizen Science' opportunities are available (we describe several at the end of the book). We believe strongly that using this book could be a springboard to this exciting and important world where you can contribute and make a genuine difference.

We want to put it out there, from the beginning: becoming a naturalist is much more than making lists and recording observations. Of course, those things are essential and of critical importance. But only when we truly immerse ourselves in these creatures' lives, only when we begin to appreciate that they share the same places as us and see them as co-inhabitants of this planet, are we likely to care enough to do something about it.

'Getting to know' is just the start; our real challenge is trying to 'understand'. And if we venture down that path, we might just discover something else: that we care. And who knows where that might take us. We might feel awe at the exquisite beauty of a fairy-wren, astonishment at the effort required to build a Brush-turkey mound, and bewilderment at the intricacy and skill needed to weave a nest of dry grass and cobwebs. Wonder is also a valid response.

Getting started

Apart from a field guide (starting with this one, obviously), you really only need two other things to get started as a bird watcher: binoculars and curiosity. The former need not be expensive, and the latter costs nothing and grows as you learn more. But be warned: bird watching can be seriously addictive!

BINOCULARS

There really is no way around this. To see birds at their best you need more than good eyesight. Working out what those tiny specks at the top of that huge tree or on the far side of the lake are requires seeing further than the capabilities of the naked eye. You could start by borrowing a pair of binoculars ('bins') until you get used to using them, but eventually you will need your own.

Today, an enormous number of bins are available, especially online. I am going to stick my neck out here and say up front that buying your own bins is similar to choosing expensive running shoes or a wedding dress: don't trust what they look like online. It is best done by seeing, handling and trying the real thing.

Visit a shop and ask to try a pair. Mention that you want them for bird watching. Any decent place will be only too happy to give you advice and help you make the best decision. If you can try them outside, even better. See if you can focus on the topmost leaves on a tree across the road, or read the numberplate on a parked car far away. Is the view crystal clear? Are the bins too heavy? Easy to focus quickly? All these things matter.

Thankfully, there are bins to suit every budget. While the really cheap versions are not worth looking at, you can find great quality ones at decent prices.

There is a lot of advice available online concerning the best 'size' in terms of magnification and field of view, but most opinion seems to be that 8×42 or 10×42 are the best for bird watching. But any configuration will be better than none.

HOW TO USE
THIS BOOK

THIS BOOK IS QUITE DIFFERENT TO MOST OTHER BIRD IDENTIFICATION GUIDES. FOR ONE THING, IT DOESN'T INCLUDE EVERY SPECIES FOUND IN THE COUNTRY. THAT'S INTENTIONAL.

Instead, we focus on the birds you are most likely to see if you live in any of the 20 most populous centres in the country. All the state capitals (plus Darwin) are included, as well as Canberra and the 12 largest regional centres. Almost 80 per cent of Australia's total population (which is currently just under 26 million) lives in these cities.

The 20 largest cities in Australia

1	Sydney	11	Wollongong
2	Melbourne	12	Geelong
3	Brisbane	13	Hobart
4	Perth	14	Townsville
5	Adelaide	15	Cairns
6	Gold Coast–Tweed Heads	16	Toowoomba
7	Newcastle–Maitland	17	Darwin
8	Canberra–Queanbeyan	18	Ballarat
9	Sunshine Coast	19	Bendigo
10	Central Coast	20	Albury–Wodonga

Male Pied Butcherbird shows its offspring how to deal with a moth

We hope this book will help most people living in Australia to identify and enjoy most of the birds they see around them. Even though we are focussed on cities, it's not just about Brisbane–Sydney–Melbourne; if you live in Hobart, Canberra or Darwin, or Wollongong or Toowoomba for that matter, your birds will be here. If, however, your city or town doesn't make this list, don't worry, you're very likely to find most of the birds included in the book where you live too (more below).

Which birds were included and why?

We had a lot of discussions (and arguments, some far from resolved!) about which species we should feature. We wanted to include as many birds as possible that live in the most populous cities. Eventually, we settled on 139 species. That's about 18 per cent of all of the birds ever seen in all parts of Australia (a total of 936 species). It's worth noting that only a handful of utterly committed (other phrases are sometimes used as well!) uber-twitchers have ever managed to see more than 700 in a year.

Remarkably, 61 of the 139 species – that's 44 per cent of all birds listed – are found in at least 18 of the 20 places included. And an astonishing 34 species are found in *every single one of the cities we cover*. Think about that. All of these 34 species are equally at home in the humidity of Cairns, the dry winds of a Perth summer and the cold damp winters of Ballarat! That already tells you something important about them: these species are tough, resilient and adaptable. That's why they have survived in our cities.

Of course, many species that are not included could easily turn up at your place. As your identification skills improve, you will also be able to work out what these other birds are, as well as some of the trickier species that live further afield, not just the birds featured here.

In fact, we want you to spread your wings and actively seek birds in other places. This book is simply the first step. But you have to start somewhere.

How this book is arranged

The largest section of this book, The Birds, contains the species accounts. In most cases, that means a description of the bird and a range of information about it.

Space limitations and the various features we wanted to present required some difficult decisions. What to write, and what should we leave out? We concluded that the most important objective was enough information to make a confident identification. Any distinctive features such as plumage colours or patterns, calls or behaviours were a priority. To ensure you have nailed the ID we also list the species you are most likely to confuse with the bird in question and point out the features that should assist in distinguishing between them.

The arrangement of species follows that of *The Australian Bird Guide* by the CSIRO, the most comprehensive and detailed field guide available. This authoritative volume, the work of a large team of experts, is now regarded as the standard reference for all Australian birds. The ordering of species used in that book is not strictly taxonomic. Most bird guides present species in a way that indicates the evolutionary relationships between the species – their phylogeny. This means the first birds presented are the oldest to have evolved and the last are the most recent. This provides fertile ground for debates and disputes among taxonomists because these relationships are constantly being revised.

While important, that stuff is well beyond the scope of this small book. Instead of sticking to a particular phylogeny, like the *Bird Guide*, our emphasis is on bird Families, groupings of the most closely related species. A family is a fundamental taxonomic category and getting to know the main characteristics of a group is one of the most important ways to aid your IDing abilities. Take for example, Family Meliphagidae, the honeyeaters, by far the largest bird Family in the country. Becoming familiar with these quintessential Aussie nectar-specialists will assist you to recognise other honeyeaters not included in this book.

For most species, information is provided on identification, ecology and behaviour, as well as features of special interest. Some of this is presented visually and some as text. These sections are described below.

FAMILY

This is the Family to which the species belongs, along with the range of birds it includes. For example, Family Anatidae includes all the ducks, swans and geese. Grebes, however, although they look, behave and live in the same habitats as other water birds, belong to a separate Family, the Podicipedidae, which is unique only to them.

ENGLISH (OR COMMON) NAME

The English or common name is not as straightforward as it might seem. Many of the birds I grew up with had colloquial names very different to what was printed in the bird books. There were Lousy Jacks, Topknots, Blue Cranes and, of course, the Greenies mentioned earlier (now known as Apostlebirds, Crested Pigeons, White-faced Herons and White-naped Honeyeaters). Australia has a rich lexicon of these local names, but they aren't much help in communicating what species you are talking about somewhere else.

For example, I recall a somewhat heated discussion in an outback pub where I was trying to describe what I called a 'Quarrion' to someone who was adamant it was a 'Weero' (which are First Nations names, by the way). Later we discovered we were both talking about a Cockatiel.

To avoid these problems, BirdLife Australia, the peak bird organisation, has compiled a list of recommended English (or common) names which we follow here.

SCIENTIFIC NAME

All species also have a scientific name consisting of two parts (a binomial): Genus and species. For example, our well-known Australian Magpie (to distinguish it from the unrelated Northern Hemisphere birds also called 'magpies') has recently been moved into the Genus *Cracticus* (it used to be the sole member of *Gymnorhina*) along with the other butcherbirds, but it kept its species name: *Cracticus tibicen*.

SIZE

Rather than providing an exact measure, we've included a chart with six different sizes, with a fairy-wren icon representing the smallest birds, through Noisy Miner, Magpie, Kookaburra, Sulphur-crested Cockatoo, and finally a White Ibis representing the largest birds. The icon size that matches the bird is shown in solid colour, for example:

DISTRIBUTION

In most field guides, the distribution of the species is usually shown as a coloured area on a map. Because we are concentrating on the birds found in 20 cities, our maps only include those places – shown as dots for large centres and stars for capitals.

One of the first things you should do is locate your place on the map below, as once we get to the species accounts the labels no longer appear. You'll need to work out if that particular bird can be found in your location using the dots and stars alone.

HOME, FOOD AND ACTIVE ZONE

To save space and make reading less tedious, some basic aspects of the species ecology are presented simply as icons. Three types are featured:

HOME: This refers to the main habitats the bird is usually found in. For example, the Australian White Ibis is normally found in grasslands and along the coast, but these days is also common in the CBDs of big cities. Six different habitats are recognised here:

 CBD

 Backyards and gardens

 Open parkland and fields

 Bushland

 Inland waters

 Coastal shores

FOOD: The main food types consumed by the species. The number of icons gives you a good idea about the breadth of the bird's diet. For instance, most parrots eat only seeds while Rainbow Lorikeets eat meat (from feeders) as well as nectar, fruit and flowers. Sixteen distinct food types are recognised here:

 Aquatic plants

 Aquatic snails and crustaceans

 Grass

 Herbs and leaves

 Fruit and berries

 Seeds and grain

 Nectar and pollen

 Invertebrates

 Fish

 Reptiles and frogs

Eggs and nestlings

 Birds

 Small mammals (e.g. mice)

 Medium sized mammals (e.g. possums)

 Carrion

 Human food

ACTIVE ZONE: The parts of the species' habitat used to find and then consume its food. This may include the air where insects are snatched or prey detected below, foliage where nectar and caterpillars are gleaned or water where birds dive or plunge for fish. Quite a few species also feed on bird feeders. We have six active zones:

 Air

 Ground

 Foliage

 Water

 Mudflats

 Bird feeders

IDENTIFICATION

Now things get serious. This section highlights the particular features you need to pay attention to in order to get the identification right. It might be the colour of the bill, legs or parts of the plumage. The photographs should help. The details include any differences between the sexes, if there are any. However, there isn't enough space to adequately describe young birds and that may lead to difficulties. Some of the birds you will see won't be adults. Generally, young birds are close to adult size, but tend to be paler and perhaps look a bit untidy compared to their parents.

Some parts of a bird's anatomy have particular names. Although we have tried hard to avoid technical terms and jargon as much as possible, sometimes these specific parts of the bird need to be pointed out. To assist you with these terms we include a diagram of a bird with these parts indicated clearly, as well as a handy glossary explaining the terms (pp. 22–23).

Calls and songs are described for most species, but written approximations of the noises birds make are very difficult to do well (but it's fun trying!). Nonetheless, call descriptions can sometimes be useful and distinctive enough to identify the bird without even seeing it.

SIMILAR SPECIES

Other species most likely to cause confusion with the current species are described briefly, drawing attention to the key differences. In some cases, very similar species are displayed together to make telling them apart as easy as possible.

ECOLOGY

Some key information on the lifestyle of the species is provided. This may include the type of habitat the bird usually uses, whether it is seen alone or in groups, and anything significant about its movements. For example, does it remain in the same location (resident), move around unpredictably (nomadic) or seasonally (migratory)? Any important behaviours or feeding activities may be included.

BREEDING

General information about the species' reproductive activities such as where it nests and when, as well as particular courtship and mating behaviours.

INTERACTIONS WITH PEOPLE

Because we are concentrating on birds living in cities, a lot of these species may interact with people. This might be enjoyable, such as visiting gardens and bird feeders, or extremely unpleasant, such as swooping during nesting. Or completely rearranging your entire backyard! Of course, plenty of birds that live among us scarcely seem to notice our existence.

Finally, almost all of these species, including the ones we are most familiar with, can surprise us with peculiar habits or have historical significance. This section describes any interesting discoveries that may make them even more fascinating.

Willie Wagtail ready to take on the world

Glossary

Arboreal	Living in trees.
Bill	The hard, pointy bit at the front used for feeding. The other name commonly used is 'beak', but 'bill' tends to be used by serious bird people.
Casque	Bony 'helmet' formed from the upper part of the bill (notably in the friarbirds).
Cooperative (or communal) breeding	Young from earlier breeding seasons remain with their parents to assist in raising the latest brood. More common among Australian birds than anywhere else.
Crest	A conspicuous collection of long feathers attached to the top of the head, often able to be raised when agitated or during displays. Not hard or fleshy.
Gape	The join of the upper and lower parts (mandibles) of the bill.
Glean	Obtain food items (usually insects) from the surface of leaves in the foliage.
Gorget	A prominent feathered structure on the breast (as in the Olive-backed Sunbird).
Hatchling	A baby bird recently emerged from an egg.
Honeydew	Sugary substance that emerges from the anus of sap-feeding insects (especially psyllid insects) while feeding. A favourite food of miners, particularly Bell Miners who 'farm' the insects by protecting them from being eaten by other birds.
Insectivore	Consumes mostly insects.
Juvenile	A young bird close to adult size, but usually without adult plumage. Usually still with its parents.
Lappet	A fold of flesh usually hanging below the lore. Typically brightly coloured (as in Masked Lapwing).
Lore	The area between the eye and the end of the bill.
Lerp	A structure of crystallised honeydew produced by the larvae of sap-eating insects.
Mantle	Area on the back of the neck.
Nape	Small area at the back of the head.

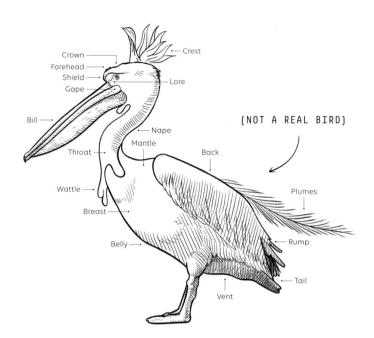

Crown
Forehead
Shield
Gape
Crest
Lore
Bill
Nape
Mantle
Throat
Back
Wattle
Plumes
Breast
Belly
Rump
Tail
Vent

(NOT A REAL BIRD)

Nestling	A young bird still confined to the nest. Some highly precocial species such as quail and waders don't even build nests and their young can walk immediately.
Nomadic	Movements over sometimes large areas without obvious seasonality.
Opportunistic	Taking advantage of a situation, usually involving foraging or breeding, when it presents itself (such as fruiting or blossom events).
Raptor	Bird of prey.
Riparian	Habitat found along watercourses.
Shield	Also called frontal or facial shield. A hard extension of the upper bill, sometimes covering the entire forehead (the Swamphen's is enormous).
Speculum	The often colourful 'window' in the wings of ducks, conspicuous in flight.
Wattle	A fleshy appendage (technically a caruncle) hanging from the neck (as in Brush-turkeys) or face (as in wattlebirds). Often brightly coloured and sometimes able to be inflated. In some species, becomes greatly enlarged during the breeding season.

THE BIRDS

A squadron of
Australian Pelicans

Australian Pelican

Pelecanus conspicillatus
Family Pelecanidae: Pelicans

Enormous and unmistakable, ponderous on land, supreme in the air.

SIZE:

DISTRIBUTION:

HOME:

FOOD:

ACTIVE ZONE:

Identification: Huge, bulky and black and white, with the largest bill of any bird on the planet (up to 65 cm long). Despite its massive size, sublimely graceful in the air and unexpectedly adept at landing on tiny perches.
Similar species: Nothing else remotely like it.
Ecology: Conspicuous and abundant throughout the continent, often gathering in large flocks. Brilliant at soaring for prolonged periods, exploiting thermals to reach dizzying heights. Will consume almost anything from birds and rats to frogs and snakes, but main diet is fish which are sometimes captured by numerous birds cooperatively herding them into the shallows.
Breeding: Famously, will fly vast distances to recently filled salt lakes such as Kati Thanda-Lake Eyre where they breed in dense colonies numbering millions, taking advantage of the temporary abundance of fish that have also bred in response to the arrival of water.
Interactions with people: Well known for frequenting places where fish are being cleaned, scavenging the discarded waste. Stories of unsuspecting small dogs, pigeons and even turtles being scooped up abound. Be careful where you walk your Pekinese!

DID YOU KNOW?
Chicks eventually wander from the nest and are communally cared for in creches. No two Australian Pelican chicks are alike; their mottled faces help parents recognise them.

Great Cormorant

Phalacrocorax carbo
Family: Phalacrocoracidae:
Cormorants

Large and dour but efficient,
this fish-focussed diver is
adapted to the ocean, but
also travels far inland.

SIZE:

DISTRIBUTION:

HOME:

FOOD:

ACTIVE ZONE:

Identification: The largest cormorant, almost completely black or shades of dark grey. Strong, robust predator. Flies with shallow wingbeats interspersed with short glides. Sexes indistinguishable.

Similar species: Cormorants are fairly distinctive, but can be tricky to distinguish. The main differences to note are: are they all black or is there some white?, overall size, relative length of tail and colour of bill. Different species often rest together, which helps telling them apart.

Ecology: Always found near or on water where it dives after fish, propelled by its strong feet. Seen alone or in small flocks, perched on exposed limbs or swimming. A strong flyer, often in V-shaped group formations. Mostly silent, except when breeding.

Breeding: Breeds in colonies, sometimes in enormous numbers, with nests clustered close together, above or adjacent to water. Develops a conspicuous white throat patch and plumes on flanks when breeding.

Interactions with people: Tolerant of people, but never tame, sometimes takes fish from commercial fish farms.

DID YOU KNOW?

The plumage of most waterbirds has a wax-like covering which sheds water easily and increases buoyancy. Cormorants don't have this covering, allowing them to swim and dive underwater, but it means their feathers get wet and have to be dried; hence their characteristic wing-out stance.

Little Black Cormorant

Phalacrocorax sulcirostris
Family: Phalacrocoracidae: Cormorants

Gregarious small fish hunter, often visiting ponds in urban parks.

SIZE:

DISTRIBUTION:

HOME:

FOOD:

ACTIVE ZONE:

Identification: Small sociable all-black cormorant with slate-grey bill and no white.
Similar species: The Little Black is straightforward: it's smaller and black. Easy. Even easier when different species rest together.
Ecology: Always found near or on water and prefers still, deep freshwater. Probably the most gregarious cormorant, sometimes found in flocks of thousands. Often rests with wings outstretched, drying its sodden plumage. A strong flyer, often in V-shaped group formations. Mostly silent.
Breeding: Breeds in colonies, sometimes in enormous numbers, with nests clustered close together, above or adjacent to water.
Interactions with people: Tolerant of people, but never tame, may take fish from fish farms.

DID YOU KNOW?
Cormorants have a fine filmy membrane which protects their eyes when they're foraging underwater – built-in goggles!

Little Pied Cormorant

Microcarbo melanoleucos
Family: Phalacrocoracidae: Cormorants

Expert diving hunter, repeatedly vanishing beneath the surface.

SIZE:

DISTRIBUTION:

HOME:

FOOD:

ACTIVE ZONE:

Identification: Distinctive – a small black and white cormorant with a chunky orangey-yellow bill and long wedge-shaped tail. Sexes identical.

Similar species: Note the amount of black and white, overall size, relative length of tail and colour of bill – these are the main differences. The Little Pied is just that: little and black and white.

Ecology: Always found near or on water, from estuaries to farm dams and everything in between. Continuously diving from the surface. Almost always dives alone, but usually rests in groups, often with other species of cormorant. Often rests with wings outstretched, drying its sodden plumage. Mostly silent except when breeding.

Breeding: Breeds colonially, sometimes in large numbers, on rocky islands or in trees above the water.

Interactions with people: Somewhat wary of people.

DID YOU KNOW?

The Little Pied is what's known as a benthic feeder, which means it finds the majority of its food on the sea floor.

Australasian Darter

Anhinga novaehollandiae
Family: Anhingidae: Darters

Strange, gangly fish-diver
with snake-like head.

SIZE:

DISTRIBUTION:

HOME:

FOOD:

ACTIVE ZONE:

Identification: Superficially similar to the cormorants and often hang out together, but has weird long kinked neck and strangely undersized head. Back plumage is dark with white streaks and underside white in a female and black with rich brown in a male. Often swims submerged with only neck above the water. Spends a lot of time 'hanging out the washing'.
Similar species: Mainly black plumage like the cormorants, but much more colour. One look at the weird long neck and tiny head is all you need.
Ecology: Always found near or on freshwater ponds and streams. When resting almost always does so with wings outstretched, drying sodden plumage. A brilliant underwater hunter, feeding on virtually anything it can catch. Unlike cormorants, Darters call frequently, a loud ratchetty *chi-chi-chi-chi*.
Breeding: Nests in trees above water, either solitarily or in small colonies.
Interactions with people: Australian Darters are tolerant of people, but never tame.

DID YOU KNOW?

First Nations peoples traditionally collect eggs and nestling from huge breeding colonies where these and other waterbirds gather, and adult birds are easily hunted while moulting and drying their wings.

Silver Gull

Chroicocephalus novaehollandiae
Family: Laridae: Gulls

The 'seagull' can be found everywhere from cricket grounds to remote desert waterholes.

SIZE:

DISTRIBUTION:

HOME:

FOOD:

ACTIVE ZONE:

Identification: Familiar, well-known small silver-grey and white gull. Conspicuous sharp red bill and legs in adults (black bill in juveniles). Sexes identical.

Similar species: Other gull species (Kelp Gull and Pacific Gull) are huge in comparison but rarely seen in Australian cities. Confusing it with a tern is possible – similar size and colouration – but the tern has distinctively narrow, sharp wings.

Ecology: Unavoidable along all coastal areas around the country, as well as inland wetlands and waterbodies. Consumes almost anything including discarded (or stolen) human food and edible rubbish, but also hunts frogs, small fish and invertebrates on fallow fields and grassy pastures. A supremely opportunistic scavenger, often forming huge flocks at landfills, which has driven a dramatic increase in numbers.

Breeding: Mainly on off-shore islands, in densely packed colonies.

Interactions with people: Who hasn't been harassed by these birds while eating fish and chips? They are actually watching you watching them. Studies show they follow the direction of your gaze to see where the food is. Clever!

DID YOU KNOW?

Unlike most animals, gulls are able to drink sea water safely. They have evolved special glands above their eyes which extract the salt and flush it out through their nostrils.

31

Bush Stone-curlew

Burhinus grallarius
Family: Burhinidae: Thicknees

Weird, wonderful wailing, surely the least likely urban bird anywhere!

SIZE:

DISTRIBUTION:

HOME:

FOOD:

ACTIVE ZONE:

Identification: Large, elongated and somewhat slender. Sexes identical. Coarsely streaked brown plumage, blending into shaded leaf litter. Huge yellow eyes are often closed when resting. Often lies horizontal. Hard to spot during the day, but its prolonged wild, eerie, wailing calls around dusk are impossible to miss.

Similar species: Could be mistaken for the Beach Stone-curlew, but that has distinctive brown patches on its face and wings, and is only seen on the coast.

Ecology: Abundant in the northern half of the country, but rare in southern regions, especially in farming areas. Hides in shady places during the day before emerging to hunt at night.

Breeding: Lays eggs directly on the ground with virtually no nest in locations with clear views in all directions. In urban areas, often nests in inappropriate places such as carparks and garden beds near shops and schools.

Interactions with people: Despite its terrifying call, the urban Stone-curlew is highly regarded by neighbouring humans who often supply food and water, and erect signs to warn trespassers of its presence when breeding.

DID YOU KNOW?

The wail of this bird is regarded by many First Nations peoples with dread, being associated with death or loss.

Masked Lapwing

Vanellus miles
Family: Charadriidae: Lapwings
(Plovers)

Noisy, fearless and intimidating, nesting with little regard for aesthetics or risk.

SIZE:

DISTRIBUTION:

HOME:

FOOD:

ACTIVE ZONE:

Identification: Alert and conspicuous, with neat grey and white plumage, long reddish legs and distinctive bright yellow mask which extends into a triangular lappet below the bill.

Similar species: Only confusion might be with the Banded Lapwing, which has a distinctive black circular band on the chest, but rarely enters towns.

Ecology: Also known as the Spur-winged Plover. Occupies any open grassy area such as sporting fields, parklands and vacant land. Hunts larger invertebrates on the ground. Almost always seen in pairs, but sometimes forms large flocks in cooler months. Vigorous and noisy, emitting a loud staccato alarm call for almost any reason.

Breeding: Pairs nest directly on the ground in the open, including on median strips, in carparks and schoolyards. As a result, spend much of their time chasing and terrifying intruders.

Interactions with people: Being swooped by a screaming lapwing is one of the most intense bird interactions you could wish for. Don't get too close to their nest or chicks!

DID YOU KNOW?
Greatly benefit from all the mown grassy fields in urban areas, though many hatchlings are lost to cars, cats, dogs, foxes and drains.

Black Swan

Cygnus atratus
Family: Anatidae: Ducks, Swans and Geese

Regal and elegant, gracefully gliding past, seemingly certain of its superiority.

SIZE:

DISTRIBUTION:

HOME:

FOOD:

ACTIVE ZONE:

Identification: Unmistakable. Black plumage with white tips on wings, only visible in flight. Sexes are identical (although the male is larger than the female); both have conspicuous curly feathers on the wings. The juvenile is a paler version of the adult. Downy chicks are soft grey.
Similar species: None. The Black Swan is distinctive.
Ecology: Abundant on urban ponds, dams and lakes. Spends much of its time floating or up-ending to forage on aquatic plants. Occasionally large groups may graze in pastures and sports fields. Typically seen sliding by regally on still water. Flies with the neck stretched out fully, often calling with a bright bugle-like trumpeting.
Breeding: Breeds mainly during winter, building large mounds of water plants and mud in shallow parts of a waterbody, always surrounded by water. Lays up to 10 eggs. The most successful pairs have the curliest feathers. Rarely change partners during their long lives (up to 40 years).
Interactions with people: Sometimes joins other waterbirds being fed at urban ponds. Rarely aggressive towards people.

DID YOU KNOW?

Before Europeans reached Australia, they thought only white swans existed. In fact, a 'black swan' meant something was impossible. So imagine what the Dutch explorers felt when they saw Black swans on the west coast in 1636?

Black Swans are fiercely
protective of their young

Australian Wood Duck

Chenonetta jubata
Family: Anatidae: Ducks, Swans and Geese

More often near water rather than on it, the duck of grassy urban parks everywhere.

SIZE:

DISTRIBUTION:

HOME:

FOOD:

ACTIVE ZONE:

Identification: A sturdy, no-nonsense grazing duck, typically in groups including offspring. Plumage is delicately filigreed grey with an over-sized head and stout un-duck-like bill. Male has distinctive brick-red coloured head and black belly. The female is a paler version without the red head and is mottled brown and white beneath.

Similar species: Looks like no other duck.

Ecology: Forages mainly on fresh green grass and herbs around urban ponds. Typically seen in groups of six to dozens, either resting close to the water or grazing methodically through the greenest patches.

Breeding: Breeds in large tree hollows (hence the 'wood'). It's almost impossible to imagine, but the tiny fluffy ducklings leap from the nest high in a tree and somehow make it to the ground unharmed. Their epic journey from cosy nest to home pond may be fraught with other dangers, but the leap happens all around us, though very rarely witnessed.

Interactions with people: Although commonly seen at your local pond, this grazer often ignores the bread being tossed to the other waterbirds. It gets used to people, obviously, but always remains a bit standoffish. Can be a regular uninvited guest to home swimming pools.

DID YOU KNOW?

Despite the many risks of living in towns, Australian Wood Ducks are among the few duck species with rising numbers.

Grey Teal

Anas gracilis
Family: Anatidae: Ducks, Swans and Geese

Small, nondescript and inoffensive, ideal for waterbird crowd scenes.

SIZE:

DISTRIBUTION:

HOME:

FOOD:

ACTIVE ZONE:

Identification: Almost distinguishable by having no distinguishing features. Small, modest and inconspicuous. Sexes identical. Grey-brown mottled plumage with a grey throat and neck, and teal bill.
Similar species: Almost identical to the female Chestnut Teal – a species it is occasionally seen with outside cities – although the Grey has a paler neck. The complete lack of colour or patterns on the head separates it from almost all other species in its family.
Ecology: Found throughout the country, but most abundant along the coast. Will use any waterbody from almost dry farm dams to brackish salt lakes, isolated bores, swamps, lakes and urban ponds. Thoroughly adapted to the vagaries of the Australian climate, sometimes gathering in thousands on permanent coastal wetlands before dispersing inland after rain.
Breeding: Opportunistic breeding species, taking advantage of high water levels elsewhere after heavy rain, often far inland.
Interactions with people: Frequently seen on urban ponds and will try to scavenge bread with all the other ducks, but is so polite it rarely gets any.

DID YOU KNOW?

One of the most nomadic and meteorologically attuned of all waterbirds, undertaking large movements in response to flooding events in distant parts. This led to them self-colonising New Zealand in the 1950s.

Pacific Black Duck

Anas superciliosa
Family: Anatidae: Ducks, Swans and Geese

Ubiquitous and familiar duck of urban ponds.

SIZE:

DISTRIBUTION:

HOME:

FOOD:

ACTIVE ZONE:

Identification: The Pacific Black Duck is actually brown, with a rather nice pale edging to each body feather. The face is diagnostic: bold black and pale-yellow stripes through the eye. The glossy blue and green speculum (the colourful 'window' at the back of many ducks' wings) is also distinctive. The sexes are almost identical.
Similar species: Both sexes of the Grey Teal and female Chestnut Teal (which rarely ventures into town) are fairly similar, but don't have the Black Duck's facial stripes or shiny speculum. Also be aware of Mallard hybrids.
Ecology: The urban native duck, abundant everywhere. Spends much of its time floating and dabbling on the surface and occasionally up-ending, filtering for invertebrates. Noisy – its characteristic *quack-quack-quack* is the typical sound of urban ponds.
Breeding: The males are infamous for their forced, violent, mating, sometimes resulting in females drowning. Opportunistic breeders, sometimes moving vast distances in response to rains. Nest well-hidden among reeds beside waterbodies.
Interactions with people: Well known for assertively scavenging around urban ponds. Usually the first species to come begging during your picnic.

DID YOU KNOW?

Females prefer the (less violent) males of the introduced Northern Mallard over their own fellas. The resulting hybrids are a serious conservation problem.

Northern Mallard

Anas platyrhynchos
Family: Anatidae: Ducks, Swans and Geese

The model for Daffy Duck, literally a cartoon of an urban waterbird.

SIZE:

DISTRIBUTION:

HOME:

FOOD:

ACTIVE ZONE:

Identification: The male is unmistakable, but most likely the familiar green-headed, yellow-billed ring-necked male will be a hybrid with the native Pacific Black Duck. The rarely seen wild type is twice its size. Wing window (speculum), visible only in flight, is purple–blue. The female is completely different, with orangey bill and dark brown feathers scalloped with white.

Similar species: Although the wild type is distinctive, the hybrid Northern Mallard/Pacific Black Duck has a continuum of features including bill colour, facial stripes, speculum colour and shape of tail. Any variations away from the features of the Black Duck mean it's a hybrid.

Ecology: A typical dabbling duck, filtering the water surface and occasionally up-ending. Mainly seen cruising on still water or resting on the shore. Gregarious and mixes with other species. Not very vocal.

Breeding: Introduced around the world as a symbol of suburban life, but hybridisation with closely related species everywhere is a major conservation concern.

Interactions with people: Commonly seen on waterbodies in urban areas, especially in southern Australia. Enthusiastic bread scavenger.

DID YOU KNOW?

Baby ducklings can swim and find food as soon as they hatch, never to return to the nest. This remarkable early independence allows the mother to keep an eye out for predators as the chicks grow.

Australasian Grebe

Tachybaptus novaehollandiae
Family: Podicipedidae: Grebes

Alert and aware, frequently disappearing beneath the water; an active sprite of ponds and lakes.

SIZE:

DISTRIBUTION:

HOME:

FOOD:

ACTIVE ZONE:

Identification: Superficially like a very small duck, but more delicate with a sharp pointed bill. Plumage is dull pale grey with a dark cap most of the year. Both sexes develop a rich reddish head and black throat when breeding.

Similar species: Easily confused with Hoary-headed Grebe when not breeding, but dark cap edge passing through the eye is distinctive (this is below the eye in the Hoary-headed). The Hoary-headed also doesn't have the yellow eye and gape ('lips') and is rarely seen in cities.

Ecology: Superbly adapted to diving for small fish. Found in a wide variety of waterbodies, but prefers still, fresh water. Usually seen swimming alone or near (but not too near) its mate. Rarely seen in groups (the Hoary-headed often congregates in large flocks).

Breeding: Prefers waterbodies with dense reed beds where they construct floating nests of vegetation attached to reeds, well hidden. Nests solitarily unlike other grebes.

Interactions with people: None.

DID YOU KNOW?

The baby grebe, tiny and bizarrely zebra-striped, often rides on its parent's back, with only its head sticking above its parent's fluffy feathers.

White-faced Heron

Egretta novaehollandiae
Family: Ardeidae: Herons and Egrets

The urban heron, solitary, focussed, stalking patiently.

SIZE:

DISTRIBUTION:

HOME:

FOOD:

ACTIVE ZONE:

Identification: Well-known and familiar throughout the entire country. Slim, elegant and fairly tall, usually seen alone, standing or slowly advancing along a stream, alert to prey in the water ahead. Dull blue-grey with a clear white face and sharp, long bill. Sexes identical.

Similar species: Not much it could be confused with except the Eastern Reef Egret, which does not have the distinctive white face. Often seen in the company of egrets, which are all white.

Ecology: Utilises a wide variety of wetlands and watercourses where it spends a lot of time stalking stealthily through shallow water in search of fish, invertebrates and frogs. Almost always solitary when hunting, but will join communal roosts at dusk. Mainly silent, but emits a harsh croak when disturbed or disputing ownership of a stretch of a creek.

Breeding: Breeds colonially, building untidy stick nests near or over still water.

Interactions with people: Always wary, even though it has moved into towns. Can be unpopular when it raids backyard fish ponds.

DID YOU KNOW?

Uses a remarkable set of techniques when hunting, including sit-and-wait, pouncing, wing flicking, foot raking and chasing with open wings.

Male Great Egret with
breeding plumes

Great Egret

Ardea alba
Family: Ardeidae: Herons and Egrets

Immaculate and solitary,
an angel-white wetland
stealth hunter.

SIZE:

DISTRIBUTION:

HOME:

FOOD:

ACTIVE ZONE:

Identification: One of five tall waterbirds with stunning white plumage, but can be very tricky to distinguish from the other egrets. Note the colour of the bill, lore and legs. The Great is the tallest with the longest bill, usually yellow, but black when breeding. Legs usually black. Lore (yellow, but green when breeding) extends behind the eye.

Similar species: All other egrets! ID can be confusing if seen alone (which it is most of the time) and it sometimes withdraws its long, lanky neck, making it look smaller. Carefully check the face and leg colours.

Ecology: Typically seen alone in shallows of wetlands and mudflats, carefully stalking along the edges of creeks, ponds and estuaries or perched conspicuously on dead trees near water. Also seen in wet grassy fields.

Breeding: Breeds in communal heronries, sometimes in large numbers, nests clustered close together, always near water. When breeding the bill becomes temporarily black and the bases of the legs flush red. Grows long lacy plumes from the wings which cascade past the tail.

Interactions with people: One of the wariest of the egrets, flying off with a harsh croak if people get too close. Many First Nations peoples greatly prize their eggs which are collected in large numbers for community feasts. This is made easier because 4–5 eggs are laid in each nest.

DID YOU KNOW?

Has the widest distribution of all egrets, being found in all continents except Antarctica.

Intermediate Egret

Ardea intermedia
Family: Ardeidae: Herons and Egrets

Elegant and placid, sporting gorgeous lacy plumes when breeding.

SIZE:

DISTRIBUTION:

HOME:

FOOD:

ACTIVE ZONE:

Identification: One of five tall egrets with (mostly) stunning white plumage. The key things to note are the colour of the bill, lore and legs. The Intermediate has a slightly shorter bill, always yellow-orange though the base can be flushed with red when breeding. Like the Great, the lore can be greenish in the breeding season.
Similar species: All other egrets! The Intermediate has a rounder head and fairly distinct jowls. The only egret to develop long conspicuous plumes on the front of its body when breeding. Like other species, also has plumes from the wings.
Ecology: Usually found in shallow freshwater ponds, it prefers still waters. Slower and seemingly more relaxed than other egrets, pacing smoothly and focussing intently on the water ahead. The quietest of the lot, only a bit talkative (soft *crow, crow*) when breeding.
Breeding: Breeds in mixed heronries with other herons and egrets. When breeding the base of the bill becomes reddish and the upper legs flush orangey-yellow. Its long lacy plumes are the most conspicuous of all egrets.
Interactions with people: Quite wary, flying off silently when disturbed.

DID YOU KNOW?

During the 19th century, millions of egrets were killed world wide to provide plumes to adorn the fancy hats of wealthy European women. Opposition to this led to the first major bird conservation movement.

Eastern Cattle Egret

Bubulcus coromandus
Family: Ardeidae: Herons
and Egrets

Gregarious and abundant,
usually hanging around large
grazing animals.

SIZE:

DISTRIBUTION:

HOME:

FOOD:

ACTIVE ZONE:

Identification: One of five egrets but the only one with unmistakable orange rather than white plumage for much of the time. Legs change from dark to yellow or orange when breeding.

Similar species: The other egrets! The Eastern Cattle is unmistakable with distinctive orange plumage extending all over except the wings when breeding, although many birds retain yellow traces throughout the year.

Ecology: Is almost always seen in groups near cattle on pastures and grassland throughout the country. Avoids waterbodies and the coast. Usually silent, but does give harsh *krock* and *krawk* calls when interacting with other birds at the breeding colonies.

Breeding: Breeds in mixed communal heronries, sometimes in large numbers, nests clustered together, mainly near water. Becomes conspicuously orange when breeding.

Interactions with people: Has virtually no interaction with people; they are much more interested in cows.

DID YOU KNOW?

Has expanded its range around the world, taking advantage of the spread of livestock on cleared areas. Our Cattle Egrets migrated from South East Asia, arriving in the Northern Territory in the 1940s, before spreading steadily down the eastern coast. They have recently made it to New Zealand.

Little Egret

Egretta garzetta
Family: Ardeidae: Herons and Egrets

Sprightly and animated, actively hunting along creeks and ponds.

SIZE:

DISTRIBUTION:

HOME:

FOOD:

ACTIVE ZONE:

Identification: One of five tall egrets with (mostly) stunning white plumage, but can be very tricky to separate. The key things to note are the colour of the bill, lore and legs. The Little is the smallest of the five, hyper-active and has a long, sharp black bill.

Similar species: That's all of the other egrets! The Little is noticeably smaller and is a much more active hunter. Legs always black (but not the toes). Has two head plumes when breeding (the Eastern Reef Egret is the only other species with the same head plumes).

Ecology: Uses every sort of wetland from small streams and urban ponds to mangroves and coastal mudflats. This active hunter often advances with outstretched wings and makes sudden darting movements as it pursues its prey.

Breeding: Unlike all other egrets, Littles breed solitarily in southern Australia (but in communal heronries in the north). Builds its nest on rocky islands, trees and artificial structures. Sprouts two conspicuous plumes from the head when breeding.

Interactions with people: Has virtually no interaction with people; too busy chasing frogs.

DID YOU KNOW?

As well as being one of the species hunted extensively for its plumes during the 1800s, the Little Egret was pursued relentlessly in 16th-century Britain as a prized table delicacy.

Eastern Reef Egret

Ardea sacra
Family: Ardeidae: Herons
and Egrets

Coastal skulking stealth hunter,
seeking crabs and fish along
the rocky shores.

SIZE:

DISTRIBUTION:

HOME:

FOOD:

ACTIVE ZONE:

Identification: To separate the egrets, note the colour of the bill, lore and legs. This one comes in two flavours (morphs): either distinctively all ashy-grey, or egret-white. The two morphs occur together although the grey is more common in southern states.

Similar species: More thickset and robust than other egrets, adopting a more horizontal stance when hunting. Has a strong, solid bill which is always yellow, as are the legs. No red or green flushes when breeding, but grows thin head plumes like the Little when breeding.

Ecology: Strictly coastal, almost entirely seen on rocky shorelines, as well as islands and tropical cays. Hunts anything living in rock pools and under rocks, frequently spotted waiting patiently for a crab to appear from a crack. Has a characteristic crouched, 'spring-loaded' stance just before stabbing its prey.

Breeding: Breeds alone in pairs on secluded rocks and trees in the south, and mainly in mixed colonies in the north.

Interactions with people: Probably the least wary of all egrets, perhaps due to having to put up with people using rocky beaches.

DID YOU KNOW?

The *sacra* in its scientific name refers to the religious significance given to this species throughout the Pacific Islands.

Australian White Ibis

Threskiornis molucca
Family: Threskiornithidae:
Ibis and Spoonbills

Quintessential urban survivor,
here whether we like it or not.
Bin Chicken and proud of it!

SIZE:

DISTRIBUTION:

HOME:

FOOD:

ACTIVE ZONE:

Identification: Generally unmistakable. Plumage off-white (if not downright dirty!) with black tail, bald black head and massive curved bill.
Similar species: Could be confused with a Royal Spoonbill (which is usually not seen in cities), but only if you are not looking closely. Often seen with Straw-necked Ibis (that isn't white) and egrets (that are *really* white!).
Ecology: Despite a reputation for scavenging discarded human food (hence the nickname 'Bin Chicken'), its diet is primarily invertebrates obtained while probing mudflats, grassy pastures and garden beds.
Breeding: Breeds in colonies (often shared with egrets and other waterbirds) with large numbers of nests close together and spread over a large area. Can number in the thousands.
Interactions with people: Often interacts with people: stealing food, landing on café tables and being chased by dogs or toddlers. Despite having a reputation as being nasty, smelly and fearless, a lot of people admire them. Ibis selfies abound!

DID YOU KNOW?

These birds have only become urban in the last few decades. Previously they were never seen in cities. Why this happened is still a mystery.

Straw-necked Ibis

Threskiornis spinicollis
Family: Threskiornithidae: Ibis and Spoonbills

Country cousin of the Bin Chicken, it sometimes joins them in the suburbs, but never downtown.

SIZE:

DISTRIBUTION:

HOME:

FOOD:

ACTIVE ZONE:

Identification: Quite distinctive with dark iridescent back and wings and strange yellowish straw-like plumes hanging from the neck. Head is black and neck and underparts white-ish. Sexes identical.

Similar species: Only possible confusion could be with the Glossy Ibis, which is much smaller and has dark iridescent plumage all over, but rarely ventures into town.

Ecology: Exploits a very wide range of habitats from coastal mangroves to dry grasslands far inland.

Breeding: Another Australian species that breeds opportunistically in response to changing water levels. Often undertakes massive movements to newly flooded swamps and wetlands far inland. Breeding takes place in colonies, sometimes numbering thousands.

Interactions with people: Shy, tentative and avoids people, the opposite personality to the Australian White Ibis!

DID YOU KNOW?

This species can fly extraordinary distances; one marked bird logged 700 kilometres in three days.

Australasian Swamphen

Porphyrio melanotus
Family: Rallidae: Rails and Coots

Robust, elegant swampland emperor in splendid rich blue and vivid red uniform.

SIZE:

DISTRIBUTION:

HOME:

FOOD:

ACTIVE ZONE:

Identification: Common and widespread, disconcertingly large with regal purple-blue plumage and black back and wings. Forehead covered by enormous bright red shield. Sexes identical. Long, gangly legs and astonishingly long toes. Continuously flicks tail as it moves, revealing conspicuous white plumage underneath.

Similar species: Only possible confusion might be with the Dusky Moorhen, which also has a bright red head but is much smaller and has dark grey plumage.

Ecology: Well-known bird of ponds, lakes and swamps over much of the country. Spends most time within reed beds, but often ventures out to forage on the shores, dashing back if disturbed. Feeds on a variety of aquatic plants, using its massive bill to sever reed shoots and rush stems. Calls often with a loud series of startling shrieks.

Breeding: Builds large stable platforms of bent and intersected reed stems, often quite visible from the shore.

Interactions with people: Bold when used to people. Sometimes joins ducks being fed at urban ponds.

DID YOU KNOW?

Has complex breeding arrangements; some populations are monogamous, others, well ... not so much. In some groups, multiple males and females breed with one another, with previous young assisting with child care.

Eurasian Coot

Fulica atra
Family: Rallidae: Rails and Coots

Common, relaxed, gregarious
waterbird, seen on ponds and
lakes everywhere.

SIZE:

DISTRIBUTION:

HOME:

FOOD:

ACTIVE ZONE:

Identification: Dark greyish, rather rounded waterbird, typically seen cruising slowly along the surface of a pond. Doesn't often walk, but when it does, reveals distinctly fringed toes. Sexes indistinguishable. Has a large distinctively white (not red) frontal shield and pointed bill. Runs energetically along the surface before takeoff.
Similar species: Very often found in the same places and doing the same things as the Dusky Moorhen, but lacks the red frontal shield.
Ecology: Familiar and abundant pond dweller, foraging for aquatic plants around the edges of waterbodies with plenty of vegetation and reeds. Often up-ends like a dabbling duck and may even swim briefly underwater. Calls a lot, a ratchety single *krark* or repeated *krat-krat-krat*.
Breeding: Builds a bulky floating nest (usually), with the male gathering water plants and weeds which he places by the female.
Interactions with people: May join the crowd of waterbirds scavenging bread.

DID YOU KNOW?

This bird is one of the totems of the First Nations peoples who live along the lower Murray River. Their enormous claws – used by the birds during violent fights and when attacking predators – are often worn as amulets. The claws are also placed over wounds to extract toxins.

Non-typically, baby Coots are more colourful than their parents

Dusky Moorhen

Gallinula tenebrosa
Family: Rallidae: Rails and Coots

Abundant waterbird in urban ponds and swamps, busily fossicking in the shallows.

SIZE:

DISTRIBUTION:

HOME:

FOOD:

ACTIVE ZONE:

Identification: A bantam-sized waterbird, dark black-brown above, bluish-grey underneath. Has a prominent yellow bill and red frontal shield extending onto forehead which becomes brightly coloured when breeding. Sexes indistinguishable. When walking, continuously flicks its short, pointed tail. Very noisy, producing a variety of harsh shrieks.

Similar species: Could be confused with the similar Eurasian Coot, which is plumper, but has a white bill and shield. Often seen together.

Ecology: Abundant and widespread throughout eastern Australia, using freshwater ponds, lakes, swamps and creeks. Forages busily around reed beds, waters' edges and up on grassy lawns. Mainly eats plant material, but will consume aquatic insects and snails.

Breeding: Pairs construct a large, untidy nest of reeds and aquatic plants just above the water, attached to reeds or branches. The female lays up to a dozen eggs, but few hatchlings make it to adulthood.

Interactions with people: Tolerant of people and will join other waterbirds being fed bread at urban ponds.

DID YOU KNOW?

Dusky Moorhens can undertake sudden mass movements in response to opportune water conditions elsewhere, with all the local birds disappearing overnight.

Australian Brush-turkey

Alectura lathami
Family: Megapodiidae:
Megapodes ('mound builders')

An evolutionary revolutionary,
overly ambitious ecosystem
engineer; sometimes both!

SIZE:

DISTRIBUTION:

HOME:

FOOD:

ACTIVE ZONE:

Identification: Originally called the New Holland Vulture, this big bold bird has a naked red head and loose pale yellow skin around the neck. The sexes are similar until breeding starts when the male develops a vivid yellow pendulous wattle.

Similar species: Nothing else is remotely similar.

Ecology: This rainforest floor specialist has unexpectedly invaded urban environments, moving relentlessly into towns and cities all along the east coast. Consuming literally anything, it builds mounds out of any organic matter (often taking over compost heaps) and treats its human neighbours with disdain. One of the most successful urban invaders.

Breeding: The megapodes' big evolutionary breakthrough was learning to exploit naturally occurring sources of heat to incubate their eggs, usually a huge mound of leaf litter. The male builds these to attract females that can lay up to 12 eggs each, deep within. Hatchlings start life by digging for two days before emerging, with no parental assistance.

Interactions with people: Its ability to transform a normal neat suburban backyard into a massive car-sized pile of dirt is a quintessential example of a modern urban human–wildlife conflict.

DID YOU KNOW?

The chicks are the most precocial hatchlings of any bird, able to run, fly and roost high in the tree-tops on their first day out of the mound.

Orange-footed Scrubfowl

Megapodius reinwardt
Family: Megapodiidae:
Megapodes ('mound builders')

Bantam-sized, but with big plans, these devoted couples do everything together.

SIZE:

DISTRIBUTION:

HOME:

FOOD:

ACTIVE ZONE:

Identification: Odd chicken-like tropical ground-dweller that mostly sticks to the shadows. Dark and dull brown plumage and a distinctively triangular head. Legs are indeed orange, but rarely noticeable except in bright sunshine. Sexes indistinguishable and always close together. Heard more often than seen, producing very loud clucks and screams at any time of day or night.
Similar species: Nothing similar.
Ecology: Forages like a typical galliform (pheasants, quail and chickens), fossicking in the leaf-litter of the rainforest for fallen fruit, invertebrates and snails.
Breeding: Incubates eggs in gigantic mounds, which may have been started decades before and are added to each year. Often shared by numerous pairs over generations. Sometimes lays eggs in Brush-turkey mounds or even takes over backyard compost heaps.
Interactions with people: Compared to its cousin the Brush-turkey, the Scrubfowl's move into urban areas has been more tentative. If it begins to build seriously large mounds in towns, however, things could get interesting.

DID YOU KNOW?

Some Scrubfowl mounds are 4.5 metres high and 16 metres across, the biggest constructions of any animal – extraordinary given they're such small birds! Thankfully, those living in towns usually construct smaller mounds or take over mounds already built by Brush-turkeys.

Eastern Osprey

Pandion cristatus
Family: Pandionidae: Ospreys

Superb fishing hawk, confident and self-assured, remarkably approachable.

SIZE:

DISTRIBUTION:

HOME:

FOOD:

ACTIVE ZONE:

Identification: Well-known coastal raptor found around the entire coastline. Fairly distinctive dark brown back and wings, but mainly white beneath. The female has splotches of brown across the breast. When soaring, wings are bowed (rather than V-shaped).

Similar species: One of four familiar coastal birds of prey, but distinguished from White-bellied Sea-Eagle by its much smaller size and brown instead of grey above. The other two, Brahminy Kite and Whistling Kite, have very different colouration.

Ecology: The quintessential fish-hunting hawk, brilliantly expert at diving at a steep angle, before plunging talons first. Often completely submerges before emerging with a large fish. Typically seen alone, patrolling beaches and river mouths. Mainly coastal, but will fly up large rivers. Call is a distinctive high-pitched *peoo-peoo-peoo* which increases in tempo.

Breeding: Constructs enormous nests of sticks, often added to year after year. Some are used by successive pairs, in one case for over 70 years.

Interactions with people: Becomes exceptionally tolerant of people and may place nests close to busy beach areas.

DID YOU KNOW?

Often nests on human structures such as floating buoys and telecommunications towers and responds happily to artificial structures erected to provide a platform for nesting.

White-bellied Sea-Eagle

Haliaeetus leucogaster
Family: Accipitridae: Kites, Hawks and Eagles

Majestic and aloof, a ruthless hunter of fish and mammals along the coasts and far inland.

SIZE:

DISTRIBUTION:

HOME:

FOOD:

ACTIVE ZONE:

Identification: An enormous and impressive bird of prey, flying on powerful wings over beaches, rivers and inland waterbodies. Body is clean white beneath and deep grey above. Wings are broad and divided into clear white front and black behind. Tail is white. Sexes identical.

Similar species: Adults are unmistakable, but juveniles could be confused with the Wedge-tailed Eagle, which is slightly larger. The juvenile Sea-Eagle is paler with shorter, stockier wings and doesn't have full-length 'trousers'.

Ecology: Spectacular and confident. Despite its name, often travels far inland, but always near water. Brilliant at catching large fish near the surface, but also hunts rabbits and flying foxes. Scavenges carrion on occasions. Soars far above, navigating enormous distances quickly. Pairs patrol sections of coastline and carefully avoid other pairs and each other.

Breeding: Constructs massive stick nests far from humans. Frequently abandons the nest when disturbed.

Interactions with people: Reasonably tolerant of people, but when breeding becomes extremely sensitive. It typically nests deep inside forest areas.

DID YOU KNOW?

Because it flies so high, some First Nations peoples believe the Sea-Eagle can move between the physical and spiritual world.

Whistling Kite

Haliastur sphenurus
Family: Accipitridae: Kites,
Hawks and Eagles

Familiar bird of prey with
memorable distinctive call.

SIZE:

DISTRIBUTION:

HOME:

FOOD:

ACTIVE ZONE:

Identification: Large and common bird of prey; mainly mottled grey-brown body and dark wings. Soars with slightly drooped wings with prominent 'fingers'. Tail is longish and rounded rather than forked. Most distinctive feature is the call, a loud and conspicuous rapidly ascending series of whistles followed by downward two-note see-oo.

Similar species: Could be confused with a juvenile Brahminy Kite (but the Whistling Kite has a pale, unbanded wide tail) or with a Black Kite (which has a characteristic deeply forked tail).

Ecology: Found almost everywhere throughout the continent, but prefers more open habitats such as farms and coastal flats, usually with watersources. Opportunistic consumer of road kill, crabs, fish, birds and even rabbits.

Breeding: Builds large bulky nests in the fork of tall trees. Often used year after year with annual additions resulting in a very large structure.

Interactions with people: Fairly tolerant of humans, but mainly ignores them.

DID YOU KNOW?

Periodically undergoes massive increases in numbers (often related to rodent plagues) followed by extensive movements, with large number of Whistling Kites appearing in places it is otherwise rarely seen.

Brahminy Kite

Haliastur indus
Family: Accipitridae: Kites,
Hawks and Eagles

Regal and gorgeous, this bird
serenely patrols beaches and
headlands for fish and carrion.

SIZE:

DISTRIBUTION:

HOME:

FOOD:

ACTIVE ZONE:

Identification: The most stunning looking bird of prey. An adult is unmistakable – wings and back are a vibrant chestnut while the head and chest are vivid white.
Similar species: You can't mistake an adult, but the younger bird is very similar to a Whistling Kite; however, the Brahminy's tail is shorter and narrower with a dark band along the end. The tail of the Black Kite is deeply forked.
Ecology: The name refers to the ochre colour favoured by the Hindu Brahmin caste and reflects the very wide distribution of this bird throughout Asia and islands to the north of Australia. Mainly coastal in Australia. Primarily a scavenger of dead fish and whatever else it might find. Sometimes hunts mammals and bats.
Breeding: Builds large stick nests, often in mangroves. Breeds in the autumn in northern areas and spring in the south. Lays two eggs, but rarely raises both.
Interactions with people: Becomes exceptionally tolerant of people and may place nests close to busy beach areas.

DID YOU KNOW?

The Brahminy is featured in many cultural and religious traditions. In Indonesia, it represents Garuda, Vishnu's favourite means of travelling. In Borneo, the Iban regard it as the physical manifestation of their war god.

A magnificent
Brahminy Kite soars
above the waves

Black Kite

Milvus migrans
Family: Accipitridae: Kites,
Hawks and Eagles

Gregarious denizen of every
tropical town, wheeling and
soaring in enormous flocks.

SIZE:

DISTRIBUTION:

HOME:

FOOD:

ACTIVE ZONE:

Identification: If you see a flock of large birds of prey, wheeling above a schoolyard, landfill or abattoir in northern Australia, it's likely to be a Black Kite. If dark with a long deeply forked tail, which is constantly twisting and turning in flight, then there's no doubt!
Similar species: Very like a Whistling Kite, but the Whistler has a rounded very pale tail, and rarely forms large flocks.
Ecology: Occurs throughout Europe, Asia and Africa. In Australia, is found almost everywhere, but most commonly in the north, where it eats virtually anything. One of the most conspicuous tropical birds because of its massive flocks, seen circling above scavenging places.
Breeding: One of the most social birds of prey, often nest close together, with lots of nests in a clump of trees.
Interactions with people: Despite living in urban areas, the Black Kite remains extremely wary of people. It does, however, provide a vital service in cleaning up a lot of human waste.

DID YOU KNOW?

Throughout the tropics, many First Nations peoples associate this kite and the Whistling Kite with fire. They have long talked about these two species intentionally picking up burning sticks and dropping them in unburnt country to flush out prey, a behaviour recently confirmed by scientific research.

Brown Goshawk

Accipiter fasciatus
Family: Accipitridae: Kites, Hawks and Eagles

The terror of small forest birds everywhere, ruthless, direct and deadly.

SIZE:

DISTRIBUTION:

HOME:

FOOD:

ACTIVE ZONE:

Identification: A medium-sized, fierce-looking raptor, the Brown Goshawk is usually solitary, seen flying rapidly with powerful downbeats or perched on a prominent perch. The female is significantly larger and browner above, while the male is greyer, but both have fine orange-brown barring alternating with white over the entire front.

Similar species: One of those genuine challenges of IDing – the Brown Goshawk is almost indistinguishable from the Collared Sparrowhawk in habitat, behaviour and looks (but less common in towns). The Goshawk is larger, has a rounded tail and a lower pitched chattering call (*ee-ee-ee*) compared to the shriller *ki-ki-ki-ki* of the Sparrowhawk.

Ecology: Primarily preys on forest birds, snatching them from foliage or in the air. Often launches attacks from a perch. Sometimes careens beneath the canopy to scare its victims into the open. Also hunts small mammals and lizards on the ground. Successfully moved into towns, especially leafy suburbs and parklands, and terrifies caged budgies on verandahs.

Breeding: Highly territorial when breeding. Builds compact stick nests, usually in a well concealed location.

Interactions with people: Has been affected by the widespread use of poisons intended to control rodents and insect pests.

DID YOU KNOW?

Probably the most mobbed bird of prey in the country (for good reason!).

Pacific Baza

Aviceda subcristata
Family: Accipitridae: Kites,
Hawks and Eagles

Elegant, secretive and elusive,
skulking in forest foliage.

SIZE:

DISTRIBUTION:

HOME:

FOOD:

ACTIVE ZONE:

Identification: Can be hard to see because, unusually for a bird of prey, it spends a lot of time hidden away in the canopy. A rather spectacular, large though delicate raptor with powder-grey head, chocolate wings and back, orange belly, attractive striped 'sailor's shirt' front, and a prominent crest. Females have brown wash on neck. It's oddly hooded golden-yellow eyes make it look a bit pop-eyed.

Similar species: No other bird of prey looks anything like it, and none hang out in the foliage.

Ecology: A very different bird of prey in almost every way. Spends most of its time in the foliage of tall trees searching for large insects, frogs, lizards and baby birds. Mainly occupies forest edges and parklands, but often visits trees in backyards. Call is a rather un-bird-of-prey-like thin two-note whistle: *wee-choo, wee-choo*.

Breeding: The male courts the female during wild flights through the tree-tops, calling loudly and bursting into the open with barrel-rolls and somersaults. The final act is a presentation of a nuptial gift: not flowers or chocolates, but a huge stick insect.

Interactions with people: Secretive and tends to keep away from people.

DID YOU KNOW?

Was called the Crested Hawk until recently, but now recognised as a baza, a group of specialised forest canopy birds of prey.

Nankeen Kestrel

Falco cenchroides
Family: Falconidae: Falcons

Compact and delicate,
hovering intently above
open grassy spaces.

SIZE:

DISTRIBUTION:

HOME:

FOOD:

ACTIVE ZONE:

Identification: Seen either hovering over pastures or perched out in the open on lines beside the road. A small slender bird of prey, distinctively tan in colour with black wing tips and very pale underneath. Hovers with the tail spread widely. When prey is detected, it drops vertically. Sexes very similar.

Similar species: Shares its habitat and way of life with another hoverer, the Black-shouldered Kite, but that species is grey, white and black, and usually avoids cities.

Ecology: Found almost everywhere except forests and treeless deserts. Inland birds are known to move nomadically in response to food abundances, particularly mice and locust plagues. This specialist hover-predator, with a generalist diet, eats a wide diversity of large insects (especially grasshoppers), rodents and lizards.

Breeding: Can breed at any time throughout the year based on prey abundances. Becomes territorial during breeding, uttering an agitated chattering *keek-keek-keek*.

Interactions with people: Has little contact with humans, but is widely appreciated by farmers for its pest-control work.

DID YOU KNOW?

'Nankeen' refers to the rich tan colour of military uniforms originating in the Nankeen (today Nanjing) area of China.

Australian Hobby

Falco longipennis
Family Falconidae: Falcons

Swift, agile and alert predator,
adept at attacking in the air.

SIZE:

DISTRIBUTION:

HOME:

FOOD:

ACTIVE ZONE:

Identification: Small dark falcon with grey wings and back and distinctive orangey underparts. Sexes similar, but female is larger and brighter.

Similar species: Could be confused with the Peregrine Falcon, but is much smaller, more agile and active in flight. Underparts orange rather than yellow.

Ecology: Typically found in open terrain throughout the entire continent, but also patrols parks and sports fields with some trees. Mainly solitary and never occurs in high densities. Often aggressive towards other birds of prey, even attacking much larger species. Preys on small birds and large insects, which it snatches from the air. Quite noisy, emitting various high-pitched chattering noises while on the wing.

Breeding: Breeds any time during the warmer months, often commandeering large stick nests constructed by other raptors. Strangely, the male feeds the female when she is at the nest, but does not feed the nestlings.

Interactions with people: Generally seems unaware of humans.

DID YOU KNOW?

While some pairs remain for long periods in the same area, many move enormous distances. One juvenile banded in Canberra turned up in Brisbane a month later, a journey of over 1000 kilometres.

Peregrine Falcon

Falco peregrinus
Family Falconidae: Falcons

Elegant, powerful, brutally efficient aerial predator.

SIZE:

DISTRIBUTION:

HOME:

FOOD:

ACTIVE ZONE:

Identification: Moderate-sized bird of prey exuding power and confidence. Dark blue-grey with distinctive full black helmet. Underparts heavily barred with salmon or yellowish tones. Usually seen soaring resolutely through the air high above or perched gargoyle-like on ledges. Female is larger, but that's difficult to confirm unless they are close together.

Similar species: Obviously a falcon from the pointed W-shaped wings and bullet-shaped body; could be confused with the much smaller Australian Hobby though that species has orange underparts.

Ecology: One of the most widely distributed birds in the world, occupying most habitats, the Peregrine Falcon has adapted perfectly to inner cities everywhere, treating skyscrapers as cliffs. The ubiquitous Rock Dove is ideal prey for a predator that takes birds in the air.

Breeding: Naturally builds nests on the sides of vertical cliffs, so the transition to tall buildings has been easy.

Interactions with humans: Its presence in most of the big cities of the world (New York has the highest density) is of great interest, with many nests being live streamed.

DID YOU KNOW?

The fastest animal in the world. One Peregrine Falcon was recorded 'stooping' (diving) at just under 390 kilometres per hour. Its prey, almost always a bird, is struck with a clenched foot, which stuns or kills the animal outright.

Eastern Barn Owl
in flight

Eastern Barn Owl

Tyto delicatula
Family: Tytonidae: Barn Owls

A silent ghost appearing and disappearing without warning.

SIZE:

DISTRIBUTION:

HOME:

FOOD:

ACTIVE ZONE:

Identification: This pale apparition floats silently down a quiet street at night or may be spotted momentarily in the headlights. Appears white, but its back is actually brownish-grey. Rounded heart-shaped mask and piercing dark eyes. The female is slightly paler than the male. Main call is a rasping screech.

Similar species: The only 'masked' owl likely to be seen in urban areas; all the others are much darker.

Ecology: Nocturnal, so probably much more abundant than it seems. Often patrols suburban streets searching for rodents and large invertebrates. Benefits from the rats and mice found in cities. Paired birds usually remain in the same area, though they hunt alone. However, large numbers may congregate in areas with abundant prey, such as during mice plagues. Can be found in any open habitat including urban parks.

Breeding: Nests in large tree hollows in eucalypts so may compete with cockatoos, possums and gliders for this diminishing resource in urban landscapes.

Interactions with people: Nothing direct, but they do take advantage of aspects of urban life such as vermin.

DID YOU KNOW?

Many owls die from eating rats and mice poisoned with rodenticide, a major issue during mouse plagues.

Southern Boobook

Ninox boobook
Family: Strigidae: Typical Owls

Small, stout and confiding,
the commonest owl found
in towns and cities.

SIZE:

DISTRIBUTION:

HOME:

FOOD:

ACTIVE ZONE:

Identification: Stocky and small with over-sized head. Looks brown, but is heavily mottled. Often seen perched on telephone poles and backyard clothes lines. Can be remarkably tame.

Similar species: The most abundant of the three common urban 'owls' (along with the Eastern Barn Owl, and the Tawny Frogmouth, which is not an owl), but very different compared to the white colour of the Barn Owl and the shape of the Frogmouth (especially its beak). Unlikely to be confused with the other un-masked owls as they are all much larger.

Ecology: Found in every habitat from treeless deserts to rainforests, but doing particularly well in towns where it hunts rodents, small mammals, microbats and large insects attracted to street lights. Yes, it does go *boo-book* or oo-oo, repeated in a long series.

Breeding: May breed spontaneously in response to rodent infestations, but usually nests in spring and early summer. Pairs use and defend hollows and raise up to three young.

Interactions with people: Little direct interaction, but is often seen at close quarters.

DID YOU KNOW?

All owls have soft flight feathers that enable them to fly silently, stealthily hunting their – often oblivious – prey.

Powerful Owl

Ninox strenua
Family: Strigidae: Typical Owls

Enormous and scary, calmly
perching with a dead possum
or flying fox in its talons.

SIZE:

DISTRIBUTION:

HOME:

FOOD:

ACTIVE ZONE:

Identification: Huge! Our biggest owl, with sharp yellow eyes in a defiant scowling face. Mottled with dark brown chevrons against dull white. Strongly barred wings and tail. Main territorial call is a strong deep slow *hoo-hoo*. Sexes identical.

Similar species: Only possible confusion would be with Barking Owl, which looks similar but is only half the size and almost never found in cities.

Ecology: Normally occurs in tall forests, but has moved into cities throughout its range to exploit the abundance of possums, flying foxes and birds found there. Remains permanently within its territory, which may be very large. Moves regularly among a series of traditional roosting sites throughout the year. Pairs and young are often seen resting together during the day.

Breeding: Long-lived (20–30 years) and strongly tied to its patch. Nests in huge fiercely guarded hollows.

Interactions with people: In cities, loses all fear of people and will swoop to frighten intruders away from the nest.

DID YOU KNOW?

Well known in the areas of bushland in the middle of Brisbane, Sydney and Melbourne – don't leave a chihuahua or small puppy in the garden at night. Human disturbance and development of these patches of tall trees pose a serious threat.

Tawny Frogmouth

Podargus strigoides
Family: Podargidae: Frogmouths

Well-known and popular stealth hunter by night and brilliantly camouflaged broken branch by day.

SIZE:

DISTRIBUTION:

HOME:

FOOD:

ACTIVE ZONE:

Identification: Can resemble a stubby tree branch. Technically not an owl, despite being nocturnal. Oversized head has huge gaping mouth and plumage that looks like bark. Mostly streaky grey, but some males (different morphs) are mottled grey-brown or rufous (reddish brown). Found everywhere with at least a few trees. Call is the familiar low-pitched *oom-oom*, repeated throughout the night.

Similar species: Easily distinguished from round-headed proper owls by weird head shape and mouth. The two other frogmouth species in Australia are very unlikely to be seen in towns.

Ecology: The commonest night bird in the country, found everywhere including urban parks and backyards. Hunts small animals and invertebrates, pouncing on them on the ground, in foliage or even in the air. Sedentary, remaining in the same area for years.

Breeding: Pairs are almost always seen perched together year-round, sometimes with large young. Minimalist stick nest placed precariously on a horizontal branch.

Interactions with people: Surprisingly abundant in towns, often startling people when disturbed on the clothes line.

DID YOU KNOW?

Tawny Frogmouth pairs do a lot of calling leading up to and during the breeding season. They duet in sequence and simultaneously, letting each other know where the other is.

Yellow-tailed Black-Cockatoo

Calyptorhynchus funereus
Family: Cacatuidae: Cockatoos,
Galahs and Corellas

Magnificent, enormous
other-worldly apparitions,
floating above, wailing wildly.

SIZE:

DISTRIBUTION:

HOME:

FOOD:

ACTIVE ZONE:

Identification: Massive and noisy, flying in slow motion on enormous wings and calling often, a distinctive heart-breaking *wee-laa*. In flight, appears elongated. Dull black plumage with pale yellow panels in its long tail, and yellow cheek patches. Sexes similar: the male has a pink ring around the eye and its bill is dark.
Similar species: May be confused with Red-tailed Black-Cockatoo, which has red tail and an erratic heavy flight pattern, or the Glossy Black-Cockatoo, which also has a red tail. Both are rare in cities.
Ecology: Spends most of its time extracting tiny seeds from the capsules of eucalypt, banksia and hakea trees. Also utilises plantation pines. Primarily found in forested country, but may travel over open country seeking food. Often seen in towns if its preferred seeds are available. Uses its powerful long bill to dig out large moth and beetle larvae from wood. Mostly occurs in flocks.
Breeding: Requires huge hollows in eucalypts and prefers to breed deep within the forest away from humans.
Interactions with people: Can become tame in urban areas, continuing to forage even when people are near.

DID YOU KNOW?

Yellow-tailed Black Cockatoos engage in noisy socialising in the late afternoon before they roost – preening, feeding young and flying acrobatically. When they perform this ritual earlier in the day it's usually a sign that bad weather is on the way.

Gang-gang Cockatoo

Callocephalon fimbriatum
Family: Cacatuidae: Cockatoos, Galahs and Corellas

Delightful though peculiar apparition, usually detected by its rusty-door call.

SIZE:

DISTRIBUTION:

HOME:

FOOD:

ACTIVE ZONE:

Identification: Unmistakable. Small, compact and stolid; ash-grey plumage with odd wispy crest (red in the male, grey in the female, matching the colour of the head). The female has a noticeable orange wash over her grey chest. But the call is the defining feature: the famous 'rusty door-hinge' creak: *creek, eery, crick,* echoing through the trees.
Similar species: No other species is even remotely like it.
Ecology: Not common, but is probably most abundant in the leafy suburbs of Canberra. Sometimes described as the 'the best thing about the nation's capital'. Almost always seen in family groups or small flocks, often accompanied by large, noisy and annoying juveniles demanding attention. Feeds on a wide variety of seeds and fruits from native and introduced trees including cotoneaster. Easily overlooked until it calls.
Breeding: Competes for hollows with other species.
Interactions with people: Can be extremely tolerant of people, continuing to feed when approached. Often visits bird feeders.

DID YOU KNOW?

During the warmer months, Gang-gang Cockatoos are mostly found in tall mountain woodlands. As it gets colder, they move down to lower altitudes, where it is drier and trees are more open, making them regular winter visitors to some urban areas.

Galah

Eolophus roseicapilla
Family Cacatuidae: Cockatoos,
Galahs and Corellas

Synonymous with the bush, but
now also cities; there's always
a screeching flock overhead.

SIZE:

DISTRIBUTION:

HOME:

FOOD:

ACTIVE ZONE:

Identification: Unmistakable. Sturdy and robust with a powerful wingbeat. The pretty pink-and-grey plumage is familiar, as is its frequent high shrill *che! che!* contact call. Always seen in groups, sometimes numbering hundreds.

Similar species: Nothing like it, although confusion with the Major Mitchell Cockatoo is possible. Only has a very small crest, as opposed to the larger crest of the Major Mitchell, although they rarely visit cities.

Ecology: Found virtually everywhere except the dense forests and treeless deserts. Once an inland species, it has prospered from grain cropping and is now extremely common throughout rural areas and has spread to the coasts, recently moving into urban areas everywhere, and can even be seen fossicking on beaches with the gulls. Sometimes visits bird feeders, but not very good at sharing or feeding close together.

Breeding: Nests in tree hollows high above the ground where the pair becomes explosively defensive, screeching loudly at intruders.

Interactions with people: Although now thoroughly at home in towns, it remains wary.

DID YOU KNOW?

You can tell the difference between Galah sexes by the colour of their eyes – males have dark-brown irises, while the females' are pinkish-red. The English name is a direct rendition of the Wiradjuri name – Gilaa.

Two Galahs carrying on

Long-billed Corella

Cacatua tenuirostris
Family: Cacatuidae: Cockatoos,
Galahs and Corellas

Raucous, smart and taking
over, increasingly common in
urban parks and sports fields.

SIZE:

DISTRIBUTION:

HOME:

FOOD:

ACTIVE ZONE:

Identification: Extremely gregarious, flying in huge
deafening flocks. White and stocky, with a very long
down-curved bill, has a short stubby crest and bluish
puffy skin around the eyes. The red slash looking like a
cut throat is diagnostic.

Similar species: All 14 species in this family are
distinctive, but distinguishing between the four white
species can be challenging. Only the Sulphur-crested
Cockatoo has the spectacular vivid yellow crest; the
three corellas have a much more modest version.

Ecology: Found in open, grassy eucalypt woodlands.
Forages exclusively on the ground, consuming seeds,
bulbs and germinating grains such as wheat and barley.
Highly social, often forming enormous flocks when
foraging and roosting. Extremely vocal in flight, giving
strange quivering – and loud! – calls: a high-pitched
kurrup-ur-urrup, repeatedly.

Breeding: Nests in large hollows in eucalypts, particularly
along watercourses. Hollows are strongly and noisily
defended from competitors.

Interactions with people: Its habit of feeding on
germinating crops has resulted in serious conflicts with
farmers in many regions, especially inland Victoria
where it occurs in vast numbers.

DID YOU KNOW?

Long-billed Corellas are continuing to increase
their range and numbers, both naturally and as
escapees or released cage birds.

Western Corella

Cacatua pastinator
Family: Cacatuidae: Cockatoos, Galahs and Corellas

Big and rowdy, always in large flocks, descending to forage on the ground.

SIZE:

DISTRIBUTION:

HOME:

FOOD:

ACTIVE ZONE:

Identification: The largest corella, soft white with light wash of yellow under the wing visible in flight. Has a tall, pointed crest and a blush of red around the face, but not usually on the neck.

Similar species: Larger than the Little Corella and has a longer bill and a taller crest. Could be confused with the introduced population of Long-billed Corellas around Perth, but doesn't have the 'cut throat' of that species.

Ecology: Gregarious and noisy, always travelling in large flocks and busily foraging on the ground for grass seeds. Uses long bill to dig up cords and bulbs. Sexes indistinguishable.

Breeding: Nests in large tree hollows. Pairs can remain together for decades, with relatively few relationship breakdowns.

Interactions with people: Can be tolerant of people when frequenting urban parks and sports fields.

DID YOU KNOW?

Sightings of this bird are common in Perth, but some suspect that most of these are misidentifications of feral Long-billed and Little corellas. The Western Corella naturally occurs just over the range from the Swan Coastal Plain, and is not well adapted to the city.

Little Corella

Cacatua sanguinea
Family: Cacatuidae: Cockatoos,
Galahs and Corellas

Widespread and gregarious,
found everywhere and in
more and more cities.

SIZE:

DISTRIBUTION:

HOME:

FOOD:

ACTIVE ZONE:

Identification: The smallest corella, all white with a stubby crest and just a little red colouring around the face. Has a rather short, rounded wing in flight.
Similar species: Much smaller than the Long-billed Corella and lacks that species' 'cut throat'. Could be confused with the Western Corella around Perth, but is smaller and has a shorter crest.
Ecology: Found in many habitats from mangroves and paperbark forests to open grassland and increasingly in urban parklands. Forages on the ground, consuming seeds, bulbs and germinating grains. Extremely social, usually seen in large flocks, sometimes up to 1000. Very vocal in flight, particularly when gathering in large groups to roost.
Breeding: Breeds in large tree hollows.
Interactions with people: Growing populations in urban areas are causing conflict with human residents who object to the noise – which can be deafening! A significant pest in grain-growing areas.

DID YOU KNOW?

Little Corellas love to play, hanging upside down from lines, pulling each other's tails, activities accompanied by ear-piercing screeches.

Sulphur-crested Cockatoo

Cacatua galerita
Family: Cacatuidae: Cockatoos, Galahs and Corellas

Super-smart, rapidly taking over cities everywhere, and getting up to all sorts of mischief.

SIZE:

DISTRIBUTION:

HOME:

FOOD:

ACTIVE ZONE:

Identification: Unmistakable. Large, pure white with an over-sized bright-yellow crest. One of the loudest birds anywhere; flocks of thousands can be ear-piercing.
Similar species: Any of the corellas, but this bird is much larger and the enormous crest is a give-away.
Ecology: Forages mainly on the ground, consuming seeds, bulbs, fruit and occasionally insects, but will also feed in the foliage and has recently started to utilise bird feeders. Highly social, sometimes forming enormous flocks when foraging and roosting.
Breeding: Although often seen in large flocks for foraging, this breaks down when pairs disperse to breed. Depends on large tree hollows in eucalypts for nesting, mostly within bushland. Competition among cockatoo species for suitable hollows can be significant – and noisy.
Interactions with people: In many cities has lost all fear of people. Will visit houseyards with bird feeders, sometimes resulting in serious human–bird conflict when the apparently bored birds start to chew on wooden eaves and railings. Don't feed these birds!

DID YOU KNOW?

While all cockatoos are smart, the Sulphur-crested is exceptional. In Sydney, it has learned how to open wheelie bin lids – a behaviour that appears to have started with one clever individual and spread throughout the local population.

Rainbow Lorikeet

Trichoglossus moluccanus
Family: Psittacidae: Parrots
and Lorikeets

Outrageous extraverts
addicted to nectar, heard and
seen screeching and careening
through the air.

SIZE:

DISTRIBUTION:

HOME:

FOOD:

ACTIVE ZONE:

Identification: Slender, rapid-moving and bright green. Obviously a lorikeet, but the various species can be hard to tell apart. The Rainbow is the largest, noisiest, most familiar and by far the most abundant.

Similar species: Despite its wildly coloured plumage, it is remarkably difficult to spot among the foliage. The Rainbow occurs in the Top End with the Red-collared Lorikeet, but it has a lime-green collar instead of orange (no, it's not red!)

Ecology: Arboreal and nomadic, always on the move in screeching flocks. Brilliantly adapted to extracting pollen and nectar from flowers, with a tongue that resembles a toilet brush. Also consumes seeds, fruit, flowers and insects. Extremely noisy whether flying, gathering to roost or foraging. Belligerent and aggressive when competing for space.

Breeding: Mated pairs stay together at all times. Nests in tree hollows.

Interactions with people: The Rainbow is among the most common birds seen in gardens throughout the country. Can be approached closely when foraging. A frequent visitor to bird feeders.

DID YOU KNOW?

Although seeds are its main food type, the Rainbow Lorikeet has started to consume mince put out for Magpies, an extension of its natural practice of eating meat (usually as carrion) when it needs protein in its diet.

Red-collared Lorikeet

Trichoglossus rubritorquis
Family: Psittacidae: Parrots and Lorikeets

Spectacular, bold and belligerent, always on the move – fast!

SIZE:

DISTRIBUTION:

HOME:

FOOD:

ACTIVE ZONE:

Identification: Vividly green with a cobalt-blue head, orange waistcoat and black (not blue) belly, and (never mind its name) an orange collar. Despite the bright colours, can disappear into the foliage with ease.
Similar species: Shares the Top End with the very similar Rainbow Lorikeet, but has an orange (not red) collar rather than green. These two are by far the most brightly coloured lorikeets.
Ecology: A nectar and pollen specialist, although it also consumes a lot of seeds gleaned from the foliage as well as fruit, flowers and insects. Arboreal and nomadic, always on the move in rapid screeching flocks in search of blossoms. Noisy when flying, gathering to roost or bickering over foraging places.
Breeding: Nests in tree hollows, with the pairs always close by.
Interactions with people: Often visits gardens and urban parks. Can be approached closely when foraging.

DID YOU KNOW?

Around the end of the dry season in most years Darwin experiences dozens of apparently drunken lorikeets, staggering along the ground and unable to fly properly. Although it was long thought this was due to intoxication from fermented nectar, it is more likely some sort of respiratory virus, generally self-limiting but sometimes fatal.

Scaly-breasted Lorikeet

Trichoglossus chlorolepidotus
Family: Psittacidae: Parrots and Lorikeets

Within this family of extraverts, the Scaly-breasted is relatively quiet and unassuming – for a lorikeet!

SIZE:

DISTRIBUTION:

HOME:

FOOD:

ACTIVE ZONE:

Identification: Moderate in size and demeanour, covered in bright green plumage with scales of yellow across the breast and shoulders. The scarlet bill is conspicuous. Sexes indistinguishable.

Similar species: One of the least spectacular lorikeets, the Scaly-breasted is still gorgeous. Among the smaller species, its lack of colour is distinctive, especially the plain green head. The orange underwings visible in flight are also a key feature.

Ecology: A swift and direct flyer, the Scaly-breasted is found in forests and woodlands, as well as urban parks and gardens along the east coast. Nomadically follows the flowering trees including banksias and melaleucas. Has a high-pitched, less strident call than other lorikeets, usually given in flight.

Breeding: Nests in tree hollows and appears to be losing out to the larger and more assertive Rainbow Lorikeet.

Interactions with people: A common visitor to gardens and parks. Often visits bird feeders, but due to its relatively placid nature usually misses out to more aggressive species.

DID YOU KNOW?

One of numerous parrots that damage fruits and crops such as sorghum, maize and sunflower.

Scaly-breasted Lorikeet
in a nesting hollow

Musk Lorikeet

Glossopsitta concinna
Family: Psittacidae: Parrots and Lorikeets

Compact and robustly built, the Musk Lorikeet noisily dives through the upper foliage.

SIZE:

DISTRIBUTION:

HOME:

FOOD:

ACTIVE ZONE:

Identification: Middle-sized, sturdy and mainly bright green lorikeet with distinctive red patches on forehead and behind the eye. Blends in well to the foliage, but always detectable by its constant chatter and screeching. Sexes very similar, but the male has more blue on the crown and cheeks.

Similar species: Similar to several other smaller lorikeets, but the red face pattern extending beyond the eye is diagnostic.

Ecology: Arboreal, nomadic and busy, rocketing from treetop to treetop in pursuit of nectar, fruit and seeds. Always noisy, especially when squabbling over feeding spots and when gathering in huge flocks to roost at night. Especially abundant in the forests and woodlands of the inland slopes of eastern Australia. Call is a high-pitched, shrill screech, given in short bursts.

Breeding: Mated pairs stay together at all times. Nests in tree hollows.

Interactions with people: The Musk and Rainbow benefit most from the abundance of nectar-producing shrubs now present in our towns and cities. Both have become almost complacent about people nearby.

DID YOU KNOW?

The Musk is another lorikeet not making friends in fruit-growing areas, with a particular fondness for apricots and apples.

Little Lorikeet

Glossopsitta pusilla
Family: Psittacidae: Parrots
and Lorikeets

A diminutive bright green
bullet careering above
the trees.

SIZE:

DISTRIBUTION:

HOME:

FOOD:

ACTIVE ZONE:

Identification: A small, compact bundle of nectar-fuelled energy. Mainly vivid green to the eye, with splotches of brown and darker green that are difficult to see clearly. Most important feature is the scarlet face setting off the shiny black bill. But its rapid, direct flight and tendency to remain high in the canopy makes close observation difficult. Mostly detected through its ringing, sharp *zit-zit* call.

Similar species: Could be confused with several small, green lorikeets, but the red face and shrill, short call are diagnostic.

Ecology: Thoroughly arboreal, rarely descending to lower parts of the canopy as it moves steadily through the leaves looking for blossoms and lerps. Often joins mixed foraging flocks of Musk and Purple-crowned lorikeets in the tree-tops, which is a wild, confusing, melodramatic noisy lot of fun!

Breeding: Nests in small tree hollows.

Interactions with people: Not sure they are aware of the existence of people.

DID YOU KNOW?

Appears to be one of the least abundant lorikeets, but that may simply be because they are so hard to detect, especially when in the company of other small species.

Purple-crowned Lorikeet

Glossopsitta porphyrocephala
Family: Psittacidae: Parrots and Lorikeets

Confiding and preoccupied nectar-fuelled jewels.

SIZE:

DISTRIBUTION:

HOME:

FOOD:

ACTIVE ZONE:

Identification: Small, bullet-shaped, bright green with just a smudge of orange-red and purple on the forehead. Perfectly camouflaged when perched among the leaves so can be very difficult to detect. However, will forage close to the ground and often remain in place, oblivious to people nearby. The only naturally occurring lorikeet in Western Australia (the Rainbow Lorikeet is introduced). Sexes indistinguishable.

Similar species: Very similar to the Little Lorikeet which it often hangs out with. Has a lot less red on the face, none below the bill and an orangey-yellow cheek patch. In flight, has bright red underwings, which the Little doesn't have.

Ecology: Found in the drier more open country of southern Australia, feeding on blossoms from a wide range of native plants.

Breeding: Nests in small tree hollows.

Interactions with people: Can be approached closely when foraging. Otherwise, takes little notice of humans.

DID YOU KNOW?

A true nomadic blossom follower, it sometimes undertakes mass movements to places with large-scale flowering. Large numbers can turn up in areas where the birds have been absent for many years.

Swift Parrot

Lathamus discolor
Family: Psittacidae: Parrots
and Lorikeets

A rapid, direct flyer, darting
among the flowering trees.

SIZE:

DISTRIBUTION:

HOME:

FOOD:

ACTIVE ZONE:

Identification: Slender, brightly coloured and rapid-moving, this bright green parrot is almost identical to lorikeets, but has a relatively longer, sharper tail and a pleasant bell-like call when foraging. Has a prominent red forehead extending to the chin and 'elbows'. The wing edges are blue. The brightly coloured under-tail is also distinctive: red in a male and pink in a female. Often difficult to spot among the foliage.

Similar species: Very similar to the smaller lorikeets, but the long, pointed dark tail is diagnostic. Note also the pattern of red above and below the bill and the coloured under-tail.

Ecology: Usually seen in small flocks rocketing between the trees, giving a distinctive two-note high-pitched *chit-chit* contact call.

Breeding: Pairs nest in tree hollows.

Interactions with people: Difficult to approach; has little to do with people.

DID YOU KNOW?

Although nomadic like most lorikeets that follow the flowering of native trees opportunistically, Swifties are also true migrants, breeding in Tasmania but flying to eastern Australia during the colder months.

Australian King Parrot

Alisterus scapularis
Family: Psittacidae: Parrots and Lorikeets

Big, bold but unexpectedly submissive, careening past like a scarlet superhero.

F   M

SIZE:

DISTRIBUTION:

HOME:

FOOD:

ACTIVE ZONE:

Identification: Large and unmistakable. The male has a startlingly bright red head, the female vivid green; both with dark green backs. Often seen in family groups, with juveniles similar to females with patchy red and green necks. Calls a lot while flying: a loud sharp *kyack kyack* or bright whistle.

Similar species: Could be confused with the red form of the Crimson Rosella, but is much larger and has no red on the back.

Ecology: Mainly found in the wetter forests along the coast and into the mountains, but will visit towns and backyards as it follows the blossoms. Forages mainly in the canopy, and occasionally on the ground. Despite its size, will avoid conflict when foraging with other parrots.

Breeding: Nests in large tree hollows, typically deep within the forest. Monogamous, and generally mates for life.

Interactions with people: Typically loses all fear of people and in some places where public feeding is allowed will readily land on heads and hands when offered food. A very popular visitor to backyards with bird feeders.

DID YOU KNOW?

Sometimes called the 'Tomato Salad Parrot' because of its colouration.

Australian Ringneck

Barnardius zonarius
Family: Psittacidae: Parrots
and Lorikeets

Mainly an inland parrot,
noisy and conspicuous.

SIZE:

DISTRIBUTION:

HOME:

FOOD:

ACTIVE ZONE:

Identification: Long-tailed, mainly dark green parrot with diagnostic black head and broad yellow collar. Across its enormous distribution is highly variable in terms of head colour and minor colours on belly.
Similar species: Superficially similar to some rosellas, but none have the distinctive black head and yellow collar.
Ecology: A common, largely inland parrot, but has moved into parks and gardens in Adelaide and Perth, utilising a wide range of fruit, seeds, blossoms and insects. Typically observed in family groups foraging on the ground. Easily overlooked until it flies up. In flight, noisy and conspicuous, giving a loud metallic screech.
Breeding: Nests in tree hollows, usually in spring, but may vary depending on local conditions.
Interactions with people: Gets used to people, but rarely tame.

DID YOU KNOW?

Although overall the population is doing well, in Perth it appears to be losing out on access to tree hollows to the more aggressive introduced Rainbow Lorikeet.

Crimson Rosellas love to use backyard bird baths

Crimson Rosella

Platycercus elegans
Family: Psittacidae: Parrots and Lorikeets

Well known and abundant, vividly coloured, sometimes disarmingly tame.

SIZE:

DISTRIBUTION:

HOME:

FOOD:

ACTIVE ZONE:

Identification: Extraordinarily variable in plumage depending on location, seemingly coloured with a kindergarten palette. Most familiar version has a primarily crimson body, but yellow, orange and green forms also occur. All have distinctive blue wings and throat.

Similar species: Despite similarities of various colour morphs, all the other similar species do not overlap in distribution.

Ecology: Conspicuous and extraverted, this brightly coloured parrot is usually seen in small family groups with the youngsters awkwardly wearing mottled patches of green. Mainly found in forests and well-wooded country, often at higher altitudes. Has moved happily into urban areas throughout the south-east and is a regular at feeders. Consumes a wide variety of foods including fruit, berries, flowers and buds, and insect larvae. Has a raucous *kusik kusik* screech, but is often heard 'belling': single musical notes.

Breeding: Nests in hollows, often in 'dead pipes' high in the tree-tops.

Interactions with people: Can become extremely tame, in some cases fearlessly landing on limbs and heads.

DID YOU KNOW?

The most diverse colouration of any Australian bird now treated as a single species.

Eastern Rosella

Platycercus eximius
Family: Psittacidae: Parrots
and Lorikeets

Iconic brand bird, familiar and
friendly, delightfully colourful.

SIZE:

DISTRIBUTION:

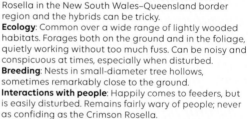

HOME:

FOOD:

ACTIVE ZONE:

Identification: Unmistakable. The combination of primary colours – red, blue and yellow – along with greens and white in a unique pattern is diagnostic. A smaller parrot and more lightly built that most. Has a variety of calls but the three-note *pee-pee-peeee* and the agitated loud *chitt-chitt* are commonly heard.
Similar species: Has more plumage colours than any of the other rosellas. Interbreeds with the Pale-headed Rosella in the New South Wales–Queensland border region and the hybrids can be tricky.
Ecology: Common over a wide range of lightly wooded habitats. Forages both on the ground and in the foliage, quietly working without too much fuss. Can be noisy and conspicuous at times, especially when disturbed.
Breeding: Nests in small-diameter tree hollows, sometimes remarkably close to the ground.
Interactions with people: Happily comes to feeders, but is easily disturbed. Remains fairly wary of people; never as confiding as the Crimson Rosella.

DID YOU KNOW?

The name is derived from a corruption of 'Rose-Hill-er', referring to the Rose Hill area of Sydney where they were first spotted by British colonists. It was first named the Rose Hill Parakeet, later shortened to Rose-hiller, and, finally, Rosella.

Pale-headed Rosella

Platycercus adscitus
Family: Psittacidae: Parrots
and Lorikeets

Quiet, wary and quaint, the
introvert among town parrots.

SIZE:

DISTRIBUTION:

HOME:

FOOD:

ACTIVE ZONE:

Identification: While the Pale-headed Rosella shares
the black scalloped back and long blue tail of all the
rosellas, its more-or-less colourless head is distinctive.
The lack of conspicuous colouration seems to fit its
quiet, nervous, retiring disposition. Call is a pronounced
chitt-chitt or *pee-pee-pee*, very similar to the Eastern
Rosella, which it overlaps with slightly.
Similar species: Most similar to the yellow version of the
Crimson Rosella, but that species is found far to the
south. The hybrids with the Eastern are found in the New
South Wales–Queensland border area and can be tricky
to identify.
Ecology: Common, but very easy to miss because of its
retiring nature. Occurs in a wide range of lightly wooded
habitats and is at home in parks and gardens. Forages
both on the ground and in the foliage, consuming all
sorts of seeds and blossoms. Never noisy or assertive,
even when disturbed.
Breeding: Nests in tree hollows, sometimes quite close
to the ground.
Interactions with people: Will visit bird feeders, but is so
easily displaced by virtually all other species that it
usually misses out.

DID YOU KNOW?

This bird is known to some Queenslanders as
the 'custard-head'.

Red-rumped Parrot

Psephotus haematonotus
Family: Psittacidae: Parrots and Lorikeets

Almost invisible as it forages quietly in rough grasses in the park or beside the road.

SIZE:

DISTRIBUTION:

HOME:

FOOD:

ACTIVE ZONE:

Identification: Non-demonstrative, quiet and private. Long-tailed, grass-coloured ground parrot, silently foraging on grass seeds and weeds, occasionally taking herbs and green shoots. The male has a lovely bright green head and neck with distinctive red rump, conspicuous only when flying. The female is dull green. Usually in small family groups, sometimes larger flocks in winter.

Similar species: Similar to a number of small ground-dwelling parrots, but none are found in towns.

Ecology: An abundant and familiar, mainly inland parrot that has moved into parks and gardens throughout south-eastern Australia. Typically observed in family groups quietly foraging on the ground. Easily overlooked until it flies up suddenly at close quarters giving a pleasant *soo-sooeet* call.

Breeding: Nests in tree hollows, but will also use hollow fence posts and stumps. Mainly breeds in spring, but may do so at any time if conditions are favourable.

Interactions with people: Can become thoroughly habituated to people, allowing close approaches before flying up and moving a short distance.

DID YOU KNOW?

One of the most abundant urban parrots, but its inconspicuous nature means it is often missed.

Rock Dove (Feral Pigeon)

Columbia livia
Family: Columbidae: Pigeons and Doves

Ubiquitous and resilient, the ultimate inner-city denizen.

SIZE:

DISTRIBUTION:

HOME:

FOOD:

ACTIVE ZONE:

Identification: Comes in a wide variety of plumage patterns, from blue-grey with double dark wing-bars (the closest to the wild type Rock Dove), to cinnamon, checkerboard and dirty white. All versions can be seen together. Sexes identical.

Similar species: Unlikely to be confused with any other pigeon or dove.

Ecology: The universal bird of city streets and downtown squares the world over, yet can thrive in almost any environment. Always in large flocks, consuming almost anything it can find on the ground: seeds, fruit and discarded food scraps.

Breeding: Perpetually randy, the male seems to be continuously courting females, blowing out its breast to produce the familiar deep bubbling *droo-ooo* call. Nests are minimalist to the extreme, just a few twigs scattered on a ledge of a bridge or building, where as many birds as possible are crammed together.

Interactions with people: Fed bread and discarded scraps by people yet even a downtown pigeon will feed mainly on seeds and grain it finds in nearby vacant lots, weedy edges and sometimes bird feeders.

DID YOU KNOW?

Almost all feral pigeons originated from captive birds kept for racing. Quite a few got lost on the way and never made it home.

Laughing Dove

Spilopelia senegalensis
Family: Columbidae: Pigeons and Doves

Gentle and wary, common around farms and grain-producing areas as well as parks.

SIZE:

DISTRIBUTION:

HOME:

FOOD:

ACTIVE ZONE:

Identification: Limited to a wide part of southern Western Australia, this smallish dove has soft pinky-orange plumage. Key feature is the throat patch of copper-coloured spots. Usually seen in flocks on the ground.

Similar species: Only possible difficulty in IDing would be in Perth where a small population of Spotted Doves also occurs. The easy way to distinguish between the two is that although both have a prominent spotted throat patch, this is at the front in Laughing and at the back in Spotted.

Ecology: Can become locally abundant, especially where grain is spilled or accessible. Forages on the ground in sometimes large flocks, consuming a wide variety of native and weed seeds.

Breeding: As does the Spotted Dove, the male performs a characteristic display flight, swooping upwards in a steep arc and then gliding down to land on a conspicuous perch.

Interactions with people: Becomes tolerant of people, but never fearless. Will sometimes visit bird feeders.

DID YOU KNOW?

The Laughing Dove is one of very few birds to be intentionally introduced to Western Australia from South East Asia.

Spotted Dove

Spilopelia chinensis
Family: Columbidae: Pigeons and Doves

Familiar and widespread dove with an attention-grabbing display flight.

SIZE:

DISTRIBUTION:

HOME:

FOOD:

ACTIVE ZONE:

Identification: Warm dull pink and purple plumage, with wings scalloped grey. Key feature is the wide circular black patch with white spots on the back of the neck. Sexes indistinguishable. Always seems to be calling: a three-syllable coo-co-cooo.

Similar species: Very similar to the Laughing Dove found around Perth, but that smaller bird has a patch of orange spots on the front of the neck, not the back.

Ecology: Abundant in parks and suburban yards. A generalist seed eater, foraging on the ground in flocks. Will visit bird feeders.

Breeding: Often seen sitting high up on power lines, roof tops and television aerials, calling repeatedly. The male performs a remarkable courtship display flight, swooping upwards in a steep arc, stalling then descending in a smooth glide. Places a flimsy nest of twigs in all sorts of not very sensible places, including hanging pot plants and on shelves in sheds.

Interactions with people: Thoroughly tolerant of people, but rarely becomes tame.

DID YOU KNOW?

The wild populations originated from escapees or released birds brought to Australia from South East Asia. Occupies similar places as the native Crested Pigeon but, surprisingly, seems to be losing out to that species.

Crested Pigeon

Ocyphaps lophotes
Family: Columbidae: Pigeons and Doves

Attractive and confiding, now found in towns and cities almost everywhere.

SIZE:

DISTRIBUTION:

HOME:

FOOD:

ACTIVE ZONE:

Identification: Unmistakable: delicate blue-grey plumage with a pinkish wash and gorgeous metallic wing patches. Two features are distinctive: the long tapering head crest, and the explosive sharp clap and whirring whistle notes of the wings when flying.
Similar species: Often seen foraging with Spotted Doves, Peaceful Doves and Bar-shouldered Doves, which are somewhat similar, but none have the crest.
Ecology: Originally an inland woodland species, but now abundant in urban areas all over the country. Has benefitted greatly from the expansion of grain-growing. Eats any sort of grass and weed seed and has discovered bird feeders in a big way. Competes with the introduced Spotted Dove in towns, but seems to be doing well.
Breeding: The loud *coo* or *coo-oo* is familiar in parks and gardens all over the country, which accompanies the well-known courtship bowing display, often performed right in the face of bored-looking females.
Interactions with people: Becomes extremely tame around people, barely taking any notice of them. A frequent and welcome visitor to bird feeders.

DID YOU KNOW?

The characteristic noisy whistling wingbeat when they take off is produced by two unusually narrow primary flight feathers – the only pigeon with this adaptation – and is recognised as an alarm call by other birds.

Peaceful Dove

Geopelia placida
Family: Columbidae: Pigeons and Doves

A pleasant and lovely sprite of suburban streets and parks, especially in the tropics.

SIZE:

DISTRIBUTION:

HOME:

FOOD:

ACTIVE ZONE:

Identification: Delicate, small dove with grey-blue and pink plumage with distinctive scalloping over neck and chest. Usually seen foraging in groups where it blends in well with the shadows. Sexes identical.

Similar species: The only other dove of a similar size, the Diamond Dove, is less likely to be seen in towns. The Diamond has a distinctive red eye ring and lacks the scalloping.

Ecology: Abundant and well known, usually seen in pairs or small flocks foraging for tiny seeds on the ground. In places with a lot of accessible grass seeds, flocks can be huge. Dependent on access to water.

Breeding: Pairs usually stay close together and nest in low branches, often close to human activities.

Interactions with people: Often seen sun- and-dust bathing, and seems reluctant to move even when approached closely. Completely habituated to people.

DID YOU KNOW?

Don't let this bird's name fool you; the far from peaceful males are prone to killing each other if kept in the same aviary.

A trio of Crested Pigeons
waiting for the sun

Bar-shouldered Dove

Geopelia humeralis
Family: Columbidae: Pigeons and Doves

A beautiful, but nervous, dove hiding in all sorts of habitats.

SIZE:

DISTRIBUTION:

HOME:

FOOD:

ACTIVE ZONE:

Identification: Intermediate sized and slender dove (larger than a Peaceful Dove, but smaller than a Crested Pigeon), with a distinctive lovely mantle of gleaming coppery scallops around its neck. Contrasts nicely with the powder-blue front and head. Sexes indistinguishable.

Similar species: Most likely to be confused with the common Spotted Dove, which has similar soft plumage colours, but the nape is spotted in the Spotted, not spangled with shiny sequins.

Ecology: At home in a remarkable diversity of habitats including mangroves and rainforests as well as urban reserves. In addition to seeds, will consume many sorts of fruits and berries. Calls incessantly, its *cook-coo, ok-woo* a familiar sound of east coast forests. When foraging in the shade can be easily overlooked until it flies up.

Breeding: The pair builds a flat, flimsy platform of sticks placed on a horizontal branch, sometimes not far above the ground.

Interactions with people: Remains wary of people, even when living in towns.

DID YOU KNOW?

This gorgeous native dove has moved into many towns and cities, especially in the tropics.

Pheasant Coucal

Centropus phasianinus
Family: Cuculidae: Cuckoos

Huge, secretive, clumsy and shy, a denizen of damp, dark places.

 **F**
 **M**

SIZE:

DISTRIBUTION:

HOME:

FOOD:

ACTIVE ZONE:

Identification: Unmistakable, but can be difficult to see clearly. Enormous, pheasant-like, long-tailed, ground-dwelling cuckoo, skulking deep in the undergrowth. Plumage is perfect camo-design, complex patterns in browns and barring, with heavy white shaft-streaks. Male develops striking black head and underparts when breeding. Heard more often than seen.
Similar species: Nothing else like it in Australia.
Ecology: A massive ground-dweller, foraging for anything edible in dense undergrowth, especially around marshes and waterbodies. In forests and woodlands remains well hidden in long grasses and invasive weedy patches. Should never even try to fly; hopeless in the air! Call is distinctive: a series of loud, low-frequency whoops, starting slowly, before accelerating.
Breeding: The only cuckoo in the country that raises its own young. Nests deep inside damp thickets. The juveniles look like baby dinosaurs.
Interactions with people: Tries to avoid people. Shy and retiring, but nonetheless remarkably abundant in urban areas throughout its distribution.

DID YOU KNOW?

Unexpectedly, the male Pheasant Coucal is responsible for most of the nest building, incubation and child-care duties (cuckoos normally don't raise their own young).

Eastern Koel

Eudynamys orientali
Family: Cuculidae: Cuckoos

Secretive and difficult to see,
but the monotonous,
exasperating, calls are
unmissable.

SIZE:

DISTRIBUTION:

HOME:

FOOD:

ACTIVE ZONE:

Identification: Large, but remains hidden in the canopy. Male is glossy blue-black with a glaring red eye. The female is mottled greys and browns, perfect camouflage within the foliage. Call is utterly distinctive; very loud endlessly repeated two-note: *oo-ooo, oo-ooo*, heard day and night during spring.

Similar species: Could be mistaken for a Spangled Drongo (though these migratory species tend not to overlap during their time in Australia) or possibly a Torresian Crow or Satin Bowerbird from a distance. But the call is definitive.

Ecology: Migratory, arriving from New Guinea and Indonesia around September (maybe even earlier). Mainly forages for fruit in the foliage, but sometimes swallows nestlings, skinks and even small birds.

Breeding: Lays its eggs in nests of many species including Magpie-larks, figbirds and friarbirds. The male uses his *ko-el* call to alert females to a potential nest. The female has a distinctive ascending *wurroo* call given as part of a duet with the male.

Interactions with people: Its habit of calling incessantly, sometimes throughout the night, can drive people to distraction while trying to sleep.

DID YOU KNOW?

There are huge differences in the distances these birds travel to breed, with some remaining in the far tropical north while others fly as far south as Melbourne, a relatively recent expansion of range.

Channel-billed Cuckoo

Scythrops novaehollandiae
Family: Cuculidae: Cuckoos

Closest thing we have to a living pterodactyl, the world's largest cuckoo.

SIZE:

DISTRIBUTION:

HOME:

FOOD:

ACTIVE ZONE:

Identification: Unmistakable; gigantic, pugnacious and ear-piercingly loud. Usually seen flying high overhead in pairs, calling often and with a disturbing intensity. Very noisy, producing a series of harsh, grating: *york-york* or cackling *car-car-car* sounds which can be heard over long distances.

Similar species: Could be confused with a toucan or hornbill, but these are very unlikely in Australia, unless they escaped from a zoo!

Ecology: Forages mainly on fruit high in the foliage, but will scoff any lizard, tree frog or baby bird it chances upon. Migrates from the islands north of Australia during September and October, and leaves around March.

Breeding: Lays its eggs mainly in the nests of crows, ravens and currawongs. May be the only cuckoo that returns to the parasitised nest once its offspring have fledged and the family then migrate north together.

Interactions with people: Widely known as Storm-birds because they often precede the tropical wet season; their arrival has been an important calendar marker for many First Nations peoples in the tropics.

DID YOU KNOW?

This species has benefitted from the expansion of crows and ravens in urban areas of Australia. By laying their eggs in the nests of these increasingly common birds, Channnel-bill numbers have risen steadily.

Laughing Kookaburra

Dacelo novaeguinae
Family: Alcedinidae: Kingfishers

The renowned Aussie icon, the Laughing Kookaburra is charming, familiar and much loved.

SIZE:

DISTRIBUTION:

HOME:

FOOD:

ACTIVE ZONE:

Identification: Do you really need any help with this one? Absolutely unmistakable. World's largest kingfisher, with massive bill, brown back and rufous barred tail. Head white with a prominent dark brown triangular cheek patch. Has a somewhat characteristic call.

Similar species: Only possible confusion would be with its smaller cousin, the non-urban Blue-winged Kookaburra which has, yes, blue wings, and a 'dirty' rather that white head. Bluies try hard to laugh like their cousins, but fail hilariously.

Ecology: A classic sit-and-wait predator, perches patiently for tell-tale movement on the ground below before flying down to grab large insects, lizards, frogs, and small snakes. Occasionally takes nestlings and eggs. The famous laugh is a vital component of its tight family ties, enabling constant contact. The explosive communal morning chorus is possibly the most delightful and forceful territorial proclamation of any bird.

Breeding: Nests in tree hollows and even tunnels into large termitaria. A well-studied communal breeder with all family members joining in.

Interactions with people: Deft at training people to feed them, even by hand. Popular to bird feeders offering meat.

DID YOU KNOW?

The raucous calls of the Laughing kookaburras are no laughing matter. They are complicated territorial calls. The louder, the clearer the message for rival groups: 'Stay away!'

Sacred Kingfisher

Todiramphus sancta
Family: Alcedinidae: Kingfishers

Common and earnest,
an emerald bullet, found
almost everywhere.

SIZE:

DISTRIBUTION:

HOME:

FOOD:

ACTIVE ZONE:

Identification: An abundant smallish typical kingfisher, with over-sized bill and large head. Plumage is shiny turquoise above and on head with a buff-white chest although this can fade to off-white by the end of the moulting year. The most abundant kingfisher in the country with the population actually growing.

Similar species: In the Top End, easily confused with the Collared Kingfisher but only if front plumage has lost its yellowish wash. Sacred has a shorter bill and a distinctive orange-yellow patch in front of the eye (the lore).

Ecology: Extremely adaptable kingfisher, only loosely associated with waterbodies. Found in all wooded habitats except dense rainforest. Usually a sit-and-wait predator of small reptiles and insects, pouncing from the branch where it has been patiently sitting. Sometimes takes small fish from the water's surface. Repeated and monotonous *kek-kek-kek* call is the most familiar, produced during the breeding season.

Breeding: Nests in tree hollows or a hole dug into a large termite nest located on a tree.

Interactions with people: Common in towns, but has little to do with people.

DID YOU KNOW?

The name is derived from the veneration of kingfishers (though actually a different species) throughout the South Pacific islands, where their habit of living on marae and burial grounds led to them being protected and venerated.

A Rainbow Bee-eater living
up to its colourful name

Rainbow Bee-eater

Merops ornatus
Family: Meropidae: Bee-eaters

Exquisite, delicate aerial master, snatching its prey expertly from the air.

SIZE:

DISTRIBUTION:

HOME:

FOOD:

ACTIVE ZONE:

Identification: Unmistakable. Gorgeous, its plumage, a full palette of vibrant colours – gold head, rich orange throat, green-turquoise chest and tapering pale to sky-blue wings and black velvet tail. In flight, the outstretched wings glow rufous to copper. 'Rainbow' is justified! Sexes very similar, but the female has longer tail streamers.

Similar species: Nothing else in Australia looks or behaves like it.

Ecology: Australia's only bee-eater, a distinctive family found throughout Europe, Africa and Asia. Typically seen in groups, perched high up on exposed branches and sallying out to grab large flying insects, especially wasps and bees. Migratory to southern Australia in summer. Found in most open habitats and often near water. Call is a clear, repeated trill, often given on the wing. Can form flocks of hundreds.

Breeding: Despite their apparently delicate features, they are able to excavate long shallow nesting burrows in sandy soils, sometimes in loose colonies.

Interactions with people: Beloved by all except beekeepers!

DID YOU KNOW?

In Queensland, cane toads are a serious predator of nestlings, having learned to find them in their burrows.

Dollarbird

Eurystomus orientalis
Family: Coraciidae: Rollers

Strange and unusual migrant always seen high up, either perched or swooping after insects.

SIZE:

DISTRIBUTION:

HOME:

FOOD:

ACTIVE ZONE:

Identification: Unmistakable. A sturdy, robust bird with over-sized head. When perched has a distinctive upright stance. Plumage is turquoise-blue with a dark head and broad bright red bill. In flight, the wings reveal a conspicuous large round spot, hence their name: someone thought these looked like silver dollars, a currency used in the early United States. Sexes identical.
Similar species: Nothing else looks or behaves anything like it.
Ecology: Typically seen perched high on an exposed branch, before swooping out to hawk large flying insects in the air. Reliably predictable migrant, appearing in Australia during September–October, from Indonesia and Papua New Guinea. Call is a repetitive frog-like croak: *ek-ek-ek-ek*, given while perched or in the air; this is usually the first thing detected.
Breeding: Nests in hollows very high up in eucalypt trees. During incubation, one partner keeps watch on a nearby branch.
Interactions with people: Seems to be barely aware of the existence of humans.

DID YOU KNOW?

The Family name – Rollers – refers to its spectacular aerial acrobatic courtship displays.

Welcome Swallow

Hirundo neoxena
Family: Hirundinidae: Swallows and Martins

An aerial acrobat actively acquiring insects in the air.

SIZE:

DISTRIBUTION:

HOME:

FOOD:

ACTIVE ZONE:

Identification: The most abundant and familiar of the smaller aerial insectivores. Deeply forked tail, glossy blue-black back and head, and a lovely orange face. Gregarious and confiding.

Similar species: Although Australia has a lot of swallow and martin species, only three regularly move into towns. All are similar: the key features to note are tail shape and head colouration. Unfortunately, they are often seen silhouetted against the sky, making plumage colours tricky to identify. And apart from brief periods perching, typically they are continuously swooping and swerving through the air. Following them with your binoculars can be very frustrating!

Ecology: Active small gregarious insectivore usually seen above a pond or resting on wires. Spends most of its time in loose flocks, sometimes in large numbers, swooping through the air, often close to the ground.

Breeding: Construct distinctive cup-shaped mud nests attached to vertical surfaces in sheds, buildings and undercover carparks.

Interactions with people: Welcome Swallows are the most urban adapted of all Australia's swallows, nesting in buildings and structures all over the place.

DID YOU KNOW?

In many Asian cultures, swallows are symbolic of feminine dignity and are thought to bring good luck. Having a swallow nest attached to your house is an esteemed symbol of welcome.

Fairy Martin

Petrochelidon ariel
Family: Hirundinidae: Swallows
and Martins

Small, delicate insectivores
swooping energetically
through the air.

SIZE:

DISTRIBUTION:

HOME:

FOOD:

ACTIVE ZONE:

Identification: Small and gregarious, the Fairy Martin swoops through the air above freshwater ponds and dams. Glossy black above and white underneath with clear white rump. Its head colouration is distinctive: an orangey-brown crown. Tail is slightly forked when resting, but in flight is usually spread and flat.

Similar species: A white rump means 'martin' and the orange head means it's a Fairy Martin. The Tree Martin is mostly black and white with a dull rufous forehead. These species often share the air space above a pond or rest on wires together.

Ecology: A small gregarious aerial insectivore. Spends most of its time in loose flocks, sometimes in large numbers, swooping through the air. Found in almost any habitat that has water.

Breeding: Builds bottle-shaped mud nests in culverts and under bridges, often close together in large colonies, the largest numbering about 700.

Interactions with people: Mainly found on the outskirts of cities and in the countryside, and readily uses bridges and culverts for nesting.

DID YOU KNOW?

The mud nests built in culverts and under bridges are sometimes occupied by microbats once the chicks have fledged.

Tree Martin

Petrochelidon nigricans
Family: Hirundinidae: Swallows and Martins

Small, serious swoopers, swiftly sweeping through the air in search of sustenance.

SIZE:

DISTRIBUTION:

HOME:

FOOD:

ACTIVE ZONE:

Identification: Small, largely black and white, with shiny black back and whitish underside. Has a pale rump, which looks a little dirty. No colours beyond a faint rufous forehead and some greys streaking the cheek. Tail is very slightly forked.

Similar species: Closely resembles the Fairy Martin, but lacks the reddish head and clear white rump.

Ecology: An active and gregarious aerial insectivore. Typically seen in loose flocks, sometimes in large numbers, swooping through the air. Found in almost all habitats throughout Australia, but never far from water.

Breeding: Tree Martins don't do mud. Instead, they nest in small, tight tree hollows and sometimes crevices in buildings.

Interactions with people: Less engaged with people than the Fairy Martin or Welcome Swallow.

DID YOU KNOW?

Like other birds adapted to the unpredictable weather of inland Australia, Tree Martins are known to react almost immediately to rainfall, collecting wet leaves to line its nest even though it may not go on to breed.

Yellow-rumped Thornbill

Acanthiza chrysorrhoa
Family: Acanthizidae: Thornbills

The most familiar, visible and urban of all thornbills.

SIZE:

DISTRIBUTION:

HOME:

FOOD:

ACTIVE ZONE:

Identification: Of the dozen thornbill species in Australia, this is by far the most commonly seen and the only one usually seen foraging on the ground. Plumage is largely dull grey above, buff below (like most thornbills), but its most distinctive feature is the clear bright yellow rump, which is especially conspicuous in flight. Also has nicely black and white spotted crown.

Similar species: Easily confused with the numerous other thornbills. The Buff-rumped Thornbill is the only one that might turn up in towns occasionally, but it lacks the tell-tale yellow rump.

Ecology: By far the most likely thornbill to be seen foraging on the ground in urban areas. Only rarely moves into foliage, except if seeking cover. Typically seen in flocks of a few to dozens, foraging methodically for insects. Sings frequently, a lovely tinkling melody that always makes you feel better.

Breeding: Often breeds cooperatively, with young from previous clutches assisting in the raising of the current brood. Can breed up to three times in a single season if conditions are good.

Interactions with people: Largely ignores people.

DID YOU KNOW?

Yellow-rumps breed in tight little groups, cooperating to build large, untidy nests which have several false chambers, presumably to fool the cuckoos that like to parasitise them.

Spotted Pardalote

Pardalotus punctatus
Family: Pardalotidae: Pardalotes

A teeny treetop tunneller,
continuously singing
monotonously.

SIZE:

DISTRIBUTION:

HOME:

FOOD:

ACTIVE ZONE:

Identification: A tiny, stubby bird with a short tail and stout bill, detected by its monotonous loud calls. White dots are spread all over the black crown, and it has a greyish back and wings, also white-spotted.

Similar species: The two species of pardalote that use towns, the spotted and the striated, are often found in the same locations, so look (and listen) carefully to tell them apart. The Spotted is very spotty. The Striated has no spots and has a pale rump compared to the bright yellow and red rump in the Spotted.

Ecology: A very small restless insectivore moving continuously high in the canopy. Widespread and abundant in eucalypt forests and woodlands. Always seems to be calling, *s-wit-PIWIP*, probably as a way of keeping in contact with its mate. Usually seen alone or in pairs, but occasionally joins small foraging groups.

Breeding: Surprisingly for such a tiny bird, digs long nesting tunnels in solid ground of vertical banks and excavations. Sometimes nests in narrow exposed pipes and other structures with cavities.

Interactions with people: It becomes used to people, but never tame. Can be quite feisty if you approach its nest too closely.

DID YOU KNOW?

Pardalotes are found only in Australia, and the four species are related to thornbills and scrubwrens, also unique to this continent.

Striated Pardalote

Pardalotus striatus
Family: Pardalotidae: Pardalotes

A tiny canopy dweller, systematically searching through the foliage.

SIZE:

DISTRIBUTION:

HOME:

FOOD:

ACTIVE ZONE:

Identification: A tiny, stubby bird with a short tail and stout bill, usually detected by monotonous and surprisingly loud calls. Back plumage is smooth browny-grey with black crown and prominent yellow and white bar above the eyes.

Similar species: Striated and Spotted Pardalotes typically occur together, but can be separated by their calls and whether their plumage is spotted or not.

Ecology: A small restless insectivore moving continuously as it gleans insects high in the canopy. Found in eucalypt forest and woodlands everywhere. Calls loudly and repeatedly and sometimes continuously, a sequence of 2–4 distinct notes: *wit-wit* or *witta-witta*. Usually seen alone or in pairs, but also joins feeding flocks of different species. Occasionally forms flocks of hundreds during large-scale migratory movements across the country or between Tasmania and mainland Australia.

Breeding: Excavates long nesting tunnels in cliff faces and excavations. Sometimes nests in pipes and other structures with cavities.

Interactions with people: Tends to ignore people.

DID YOU KNOW?

Pardalotes play a significant role in controlling lerp infestations in the eucalypt forests of Australia. Defending lerp-rich patches of foliage from raids by honeyeaters can take up a lot of the small pardalote's time.

'Is that really me?' A Striated Pardalote visiting a bird bath

Superb Fairy-wren

Malurus cyaneus
Family: Maluridae: Fairy-wrens

A tiny, vivacious, group-loving sprite with a complicated social life.

SIZE:

DISTRIBUTION:

HOME:

FOOD:

ACTIVE ZONE:

Identification: Lively and familiar, bouncing around in family groups. Ventures tentatively out from the thickets to forage in the open. Most are dull brown, but the male moults into a gorgeous blue uniform when breeding. Juveniles have no blue in the tail and a yellow gape.

Similar species: The male is easy to distinguish but juveniles, females and non-breeding males that make up most of the groups can be tricky. Look for the colour of the tail and the lores. In the Superb, the dominant male loses his bright colours outside the breeding season, but retains his blue tail. The adult female has a pale blue tail.

Ecology: An active insectivore, gleaning from the foliage or on open ground. Always seen in family groups, with a single patriarchal colourful male presiding over a clan consisting of a few to a dozen uncoloured females and juveniles. Poor flyers.

Breeding: Quintessential communal breeder. Offspring from earlier breeding seasons assist in the raising of the next batch of hatchlings. Only one adult male in the group is fully coloured.

Interactions with people: Not common in urban gardens, but always welcome.

DID YOU KNOW?

Fairy-wrens are infamous for having most of the offspring in a 'family group' fathered by males from outside their territory. The world record holder, with an average of about 80 per cent of young unrelated to the resident male.

Splendid Fairy-wren

Malurus splendens
Family: Maluridae: Fairy-wrens

Gorgeous and widespread, the Splendid is the inland fairy-wren.

SIZE:

DISTRIBUTION:

HOME:

FOOD:

ACTIVE ZONE:

Identification: The breeding male is stunning and unmistakable, body plumage a gleaming rich purple-blue with a black stripe through the eye and across the breast. When not breeding, the tail and wings retain the blue. The adult female has a light blue tail and lores paler than the bill. Juvenile Splendids have a blue wash through the tail and a yellow gape.

Similar species: The male Splendid Fairy-wren is fairly straightforward to distinguish but females, juveniles and pre-breeding males can be tricky. Look for the colour of the tail and the lores.

Ecology: An active insectivore seeking food from among the foliage or open ground near dense vegetation, but never venturing far from cover. Always found in family groups, with a single brightly coloured male.

Breeding: Breeds communally, with previous offspring assisting with the raising of the next brood. The dominant male in the group is fully coloured while breeding, with all other members dull brown and cream.

Interactions with people: Common inland and in south-western Australia, but rarely seen right in town. Check the reserves and parks on the outskirts.

DID YOU KNOW?

Males undergo two moults each year, with their splendid blue plumage only present when breeding. Once this intense period is over, the birds quickly moult into a drab brown, like all of the other birds in the fairy-wren group.

Red-backed Fairy-wren

Malurus melanocephalus
Family: Maluridae: Fairy-wrens

Startlingly beautiful, a scarlet and pitch-black sprite.

M   F

SIZE:

DISTRIBUTION:

HOME:

FOOD:

ACTIVE ZONE:

Identification: A breeding male is spectacular and unmissable: unmissably conspicuous in its vivid red and black uniform. However, when not breeding everyone in the group is remarkably dull with no colour anywhere. Virtually impossible to separate ages and sexes at non-breeding stages. Juveniles have no blue on tail (like Superb) and are buffer underneath.

Similar species: All breeding male fairy-wrens are easy to identify but juveniles, females and pre-breeding males can be tricky. And Red-backs are possibly the worst!

Ecology: Busy and secretive, remaining within the dense understorey most of the time. Insectivore gleaning tiny insects from the foliage or on open ground, but won't venture far from cover. Always seen in small flocks, with a single colourful male in charge.

Breeding: Breeds cooperatively, with previous offspring helping raise the latest chicks. Only the dominant male in the group becomes coloured, with all other members remaining dull brown and cream.

Interactions with people: Rare in the suburbs, but usually found in nearby natural bush.

DID YOU KNOW?

Red-backs are the smallest fairy-wrens and possibly the lightest of all Australian birds, weighing a tiny 5–10 grams (about the same weight as a small strawberry).

Variegated Fairy-wren

Malurus lamberti
Family: Maluridae: Fairy-wrens

Shy and secretive, preferring to stay hidden within the understorey.

SIZE:

DISTRIBUTION:

HOME:

FOOD:

ACTIVE ZONE:

Identification: The breeding male has a sky-blue helmet extending down to his cheeks, surrounded by a black bib. Back is rich chestnut brown. When not breeding, the male retains only his blue tail. The adult female has a similar blue tail, and a dark rufous lore, which is black in the male. The juvenile has a blue tail, but most distinctively a dark lore.

Similar species: The breeding male Variegated is obvious, but identifying the juvenile, female and pre-breeding male can be tricky. Look for the tail and lore colours. The most likely confusion in urban areas will be with the non-breeding Superb Fairy-wren, which has a colourless lore and much darker blue on its tail.

Ecology: This is the least public fairy-wren, reluctant to move away from the cover of dense vegetation. Always seen in family groups. Has the broadest distribution of all fairy-wrens, spanning the entire continent.

Breeding: Like other fairy-wrens is a communal breeder, with the whole group helping out at breeding time.

Interactions with people: Rarely seen in backyards and secretive at the best of times. They even call less than other fairy-wrens so you will need to be patient.

DID YOU KNOW?

Typically non-monogamous domestic affairs as per all the fairy-wrens, though the breeding pair remain together. Like other fairy-wrens, the male courts potential partners by presenting bouquets of flower petals – in this case, yellow ones.

Singing Honeyeater

Gavicalis virescens
Family: Meliphagidae:
Honeyeaters, Miners,
Wattlebirds and Friarbirds

The inland honeyeater flits
though the sparse vegetation
of the outback.

SIZE:

DISTRIBUTION:

HOME:

FOOD:

ACTIVE ZONE:

Identification: Rather dull grey-brown medium-sized honeyeater with pale underparts lightly streaked. Most distinctive feature is the black mask over the eyes and beyond.

Similar species: Comparable to several similarly-sized honeyeaters, but their distributions don't overlap and none are found in towns.

Ecology: The most widely distributed honeyeater, found everywhere except the coastal forest of the tropics and eastern coast. Mainly seen alone or in small family groups. Rather omnivorous, consuming caterpillars, berries, all sorts of insects, as well as nectar. The name is a bit misleading; their varied calls are not very musical, the most common being a simple *prrt*.

Breeding: Like many species adapted to the unpredictable inland, can breed whenever conditions are suitable. In urban areas, however, they breed mostly in late spring.

Interactions with humans: Remarkably, it has become one of the most common birds seen throughout the suburbs of Perth, taking advantage – like many other species – of all the nectar-bearing plants.

DID YOU KNOW?

This bird's common name alludes to the evolution of complex voiceboxes in all songbirds occuring in Australia (Gondwana actually), before it spread to the rest of the world. But, frankly, this species isn't that good a songster.

White-plumed Honeyeater

Ptilotula penicillata
Family: Meliphagidae:
Honeyeaters, Miners, Wattlebirds
and Friarbirds

Familiar, common and cheerful
honeyeater found throughout
the inland.

SIZE:

DISTRIBUTION:

HOME:

FOOD:

ACTIVE ZONE:

Identification: Small olive-green honeyeater (the 'Greenies' of my youth, mentioned earlier in the book) with noticeable white stripe on each side of the neck, fastidiously searching through the foliage while constantly calling with a distinctive bright *chip-chip-a-wee*. Sexes identical.

Similar species: Plenty of possibilities for confusion with other similarly-sized honeyeaters, but the conspicuous white stripe on the neck combined with the bright yellow face make it distinctive.

Ecology: Gregarious and extraverted, often chasing and bickering, accompanied by vigorous calling. Feeds on nectar and the insects it encounters, frequently snatching them from the air. Very fond of lerps as well.

Breeding: Builds dainty purse-like nests of fine grasses and cobwebs suspended from twigs on the very ends of branches of eucalypts, presumably to reduce the risk of predation.

Interactions with people: Has moved into towns to take advantage of the many nectar-producing plants, but is also one of the few honeyeaters to wholeheartedly exploit a range of foreign garden plants.

DID YOU KNOW?

One of the most sedentary honeyeaters, rarely moving more than 10 kilometres in its life.

Lewin's Honeyeater
in a grevillea

Lewin's Honeyeater

Meliphaga lewinii
Family: Meliphagidae:
Honeyeaters, Miners, Wattlebirds
and Friarbirds

Noisy, confident honeyeater
of forests and leafy suburbs.

SIZE:

DISTRIBUTION:

HOME:

FOOD:

ACTIVE ZONE:

Identification: One of the larger small honeyeaters, but more slender than friarbirds and wattlebirds. It often moves about within the denser foliage, its dark olive-green plumage offering the perfect camouflage. Usually detected initially by its rapid-fire *chi-chi-chi-chi* chatter repeated incessantly. The large half disc of dull yellow on the cheek is diagnostic.

Similar species: The two very similar-looking honeyeaters from the forests of northern Queensland are unlikely to be seen in towns.

Ecology: Active and alert, moving through the foliage at all heights, but will sometimes pursue large insects out of cover and onto the ground. Usually found in flocks of up to 10 birds. Prefers the denser forests with thick cover, but will venture into gardens and parks.

Breeding: Breeds in the warmer months, the pair building a small, compact nest bound together with spider's web. Both partners raise the offspring.

Interactions with people: In urban areas can become quite tame. Often visits feeders with sugary offerings, but will, inexplicably, eat bread.

DID YOU KNOW?

The name comes from John Lewin, who was an English-born naturalist and illustrator working in the colony of New South Wales in the early 1800s. He was the first professional artist working in Australia.

Yellow-faced Honeyeater

Caligavis chrysops
Family: Meliphagidae: Honeyeaters, Miners, Wattlebirds and Friarbirds

Abundant migratory honeyeater, constantly busy pursuing insects and sipping nectar.

SIZE:

DISTRIBUTION:

HOME:

FOOD:

ACTIVE ZONE:

Identification: Dull small browny-grey honeyeater with a distinctive vivid black–yellow–black facial stripe. Abundant and widespread. Call is a bright, pleasant *chirry chirry-up* uttered throughout the day. The sexes are identical.

Similar species: Plenty of possibilities for confusion with other similarly sized honeyeaters, but the conspicuous bold facial pattern is distinctive.

Ecology: Gregarious and extraverted, often chasing and bickering with other birds, accompanied by lots of calls. Feeds on nectar and insects, including lerps and honeydew. Also adept at snatching flying insects from the air.

Breeding: Builds fine whiskey-glass-shaped nests of fine grasses and cobwebs. The monogamous pairs typically have three breeding attempts each year. While breeding, the birds are highly aggressive toward almost every other species coming near the nest.

Interactions with people: Enjoys the many nectar-producing flowers present in gardens and backyards, but otherwise is oblivious to people.

DID YOU KNOW?

Vast numbers of these birds undertake south to north migrations during the colder months (over 100 000 were recorded in one day passing Hastings Point in New South Wales).

Scarlet Honeyeater

Myzomela sanguinolenta
Family: Meliphagidae:
Honeyeaters, Miners, Wattlebirds
and Friarbirds

Gorgeous and busy, flitting
through the foliage from
flower to flower.

F

M

SIZE:

DISTRIBUTION:

HOME:

FOOD:

ACTIVE ZONE:

Identification: Distinctively small. The male is bright red and black, while the female is dull brown with just a light wash of red on the face. Long down-curved bill, synonymous with nectar feeding.

Similar species: Most similar to the Red-headed Honeyeater from the Top End, but the two don't overlap. For a moment, could be confused with the Mistletoebird, but that species has a black, not red, head.

Ecology: Busy and industrious tiny red honeyeater, found in a wide variety of habitats where it searches continuously for nectar and insects among the foliage. Visits parks and backyards wherever nectar-producing plants are in flower. Mainly seen alone or in pairs, but sometimes in large mobile flocks. Has a loud, sharp fluctuating call: *oodill-oodill-oo*.

Breeding: The female constructs a tiny neat cut of shredded bark held together with cobwebs. Almost always attempts to raise multiple clutches each year.

Interactions with humans: Happily visits houseyards to exploit any nectar, but more or less pretends people don't exist.

DID YOU KNOW?

Has periodic explosions in numbers ('irruptions') resulting in vast numbers of these gorgeous birds flooding some areas.

Brown Honeyeater

Lichmera indistincta
Family: Meliphagidae:
Honeyeaters, Miners, Wattlebirds
and Friarbirds

Small, active and spirited,
constantly singing, but rather
dull plumage.

SIZE:

DISTRIBUTION:

HOME:

FOOD:

ACTIVE ZONE:

Identification: Seriously nondescript. If it's a small, busy honeyeater with no distinctive features, it's probably a Brown. Has a pale yellow gape and triangle behind the eye, but these features are difficult to detect. Its loud, clear calls are the most reliable feature.

Similar species: Could easily be confused with the female Scarlet or Red-headed honeyeaters though both have reddish faces. The Dusky Honeyeater is very similar, but darker all over. Neither Red-headeds or Duskys occur in cities.

Ecology: Lives in many habitats, from mangroves and rainforest edges to arid scrublands, but avoids tall forests. Restlessly moves through the foliage, calling incessantly, delivering a remarkable collection of calls including a staccato *ch-ch-ch* and complex, melodious songs.

Breeding: Can breed at any time of the year though usually in spring. Builds a tiny nest suspended in the fine outer branches.

Interactions with people: Often ignores people while going about its business.

DID YOU KNOW?

Inland populations of this widespread species move nomadically in response to local food availability. In wetter coastal areas and mangroves, however, it rarely leaves its small home range.

New Holland Honeyeater

Phylidonyris novaehollandiae
Family: Meliphagidae:
Honeyeaters, Miners, Wattlebirds
and Friarbirds

Belligerent, energetic and boldly patterned honeyeater, blasting out calls from a high perch.

SIZE:

DISTRIBUTION:

HOME:

FOOD:

ACTIVE ZONE:

Identification: Abundant and conspicuous, with striking yellow and black wings and vivid vertical zebra stripes down the front. The yellow on its tail and wings is very evident in flight.

Similar species: Only real risk of misidentification would be with the White-cheeked Honeyeater, but the White-cheeked has a large fan-shaped white cheek patch, and is much less likely to be seen in suburban gardens.

Ecology: Has a serious sugar addiction! Makes large-scale movements to wherever the best flowering is happening. Extremely competitive when it comes to good nectar sources, with constant fights and chases. Also hunts large insects, often chasing them out into the open.

Breeding: Breeding territories, timing of breeding and population abundance are strongly associated with nectar availability. Pairs seem to be long-lasting. The female tends to do most of the incubation and rearing of the nestlings, while the male is preoccupied with driving away intruders trying to steal nectar.

Interactions with people: Mostly ignores people, even at close range. Enjoys splashing in backyard bird baths in family groups.

DID YOU KNOW?

Although seemingly always antagonistic over food resources, it will cooperate when others alarm-call to mob a passing hawk.

Eastern Spinebill

Acanthorynchus tenuirostris
Family: Meliphagidae:
Honeyeaters, Miners, Wattlebirds
and Friarbirds

Hyperactive and antagonistic,
a tiny and energetic jewel
darting between thickets.

SIZE:

DISTRIBUTION:

HOME:

FOOD:

ACTIVE ZONE:

Identification: Small, busy and despotic honeyeater, never still or relaxed. Distinctively slender with a very long down-curved bill. The male has a smart uniform of rich rufous and striking black, white and chocolate with a lovely orange bib. The female is very similar, but has a grey crown rather than black.

Similar species: Unmistakable, but could be confused with the Tawny-crowned Honeyeater, a non-urban species, which has the same general shape, but not the orange-rufous patches. In Western Australia is replaced by the Western Spinebill, but this bird is rarely sighted in Perth.

Ecology: Energetic nectar addict, continuously chasing and displacing competitors of any species. Particularly fond of heath plants and dense shrubs, but also takes insects and spiders. Has a distinctive loud sharp whistle call: *ting, ting, ting*. Follows the flowering plants nomadically and typically moves into towns in winter where many cultivars continue to produce nectar.

Breeding: The female constructs a deep neat cup nest hidden within the foliage of a dense shrub.

Interactions with people: A welcome if indifferent visitor to many suburban gardens.

DID YOU KNOW?

One of very few Australian birds that can hover like a hummingbird while extracting nectar (the Olive-backed Sunbird is another).

Spiny-cheeked Honeyeater

Acanthagenys rufogularis
Family: Meliphagidae: Honeyeaters, Miners, Wattlebirds and Friarbirds

Common denizen of the inland and regional gardens; cantankerous and noisy.

SIZE:

DISTRIBUTION:

HOME:

FOOD:

ACTIVE ZONE:

Identification: One of the smallest of the large honeyeaters such as wattlebirds and friarbirds. Greenish above and streaked beneath, but the apricot throat and yellow, black-tipped bill are distinctive. Usually detected first by its weird, gurgling sing-song vocalisations and prolonged call: *keup, kwip, kyoo-er, kwi-up*. Sexes look the same.

Similar species: Could be confused with the Striped Honeyeater, which occurs in similar habitats in the east, but rarely seen in urban areas. The Striped also has prominent streaks, on the head not the chest, and lacks the apricot throat colour.

Ecology: A typical assertive honeyeater, actively foraging through the foliage of trees and shrubs of lightly wooded areas as well as town parks and backyards. Remarkably broad diet that can include eggs and nestlings, as well as the typical nectar and insects.

Breeding: Neat nests woven with fine grasses are built by the female, often decorated with spider eggs-sacs and lined with possum fur.

Interactions with people: Not many interactions, but is a welcome visitor to many town gardens.

DID YOU KNOW?

'Spiny-cheeks' refer to the sharp, hardened white bristles on the sides of the face.

Blue-faced Honeyeater

Entomyzon cyanotis
Family: Meliphagidae:
Honeyeaters, Miners, Wattlebirds and Friarbirds

Big, bold and belligerent, conspicuous and alert with a fondness for palms.

SIZE:

DISTRIBUTION:

HOME:

FOOD:

ACTIVE ZONE:

Identification: Large, obvious and unmistakable. Its size, clean bold colours and endless *woyip?* calls are a unique combination. Bright olive-green above, clean linen-white below. The most distinctive feature is the large royal blue bare skin patch around the eye (yellowy-green in younger birds).

Similar species: Friarbird-sized, but apart from an equally pugnacious personality, completely different.

Ecology: Lives mainly in woodlands and open forests, but loves parks and gardens, especially those with plenty of palms. Usually seen in family groups of up to about 10, moving conspicuously through the foliage and down trunks, prying into crevices in the bark. Will consume almost anything edible including the contents of nests. Continuously keeps in contact with an upwardly inflected yelp.

Breeding: Nest is large and untidy, stuck into the fork of a tree or the base of a palm frond. Breeding behaviour has not been well studied, but this species is likely a cooperative breeder like so many other Australian birds.

Interactions with people: Ignores people.

DID YOU KNOW?

Known as 'Banana Bird' in the tropics because of its fondness for banana fruits and flowers.

A fluffy nestling Blue-faced Honeyeater, before its face turns yellow-green

Noisy Miner

Manorina melanocephala
Family: Meliphagidae:
Honeyeaters, Miners, Wattlebirds
and Friarbirds

Ultra-aggressive despotic
honeyeater notorious for
driving away almost all
other birds.

SIZE:

DISTRIBUTION:

HOME:

FOOD:

ACTIVE ZONE:

Identification: Extremely common and very well known. A moderate-sized tough guy with attitude and dark grey-olive plumage above and slightly lighter below. Broad black band over entire head. Sharp yellow bill and distinctive yellow tear-drop behind the eye.
Similar species: Easily confused with the mostly non-urban Yellow-throated Miner, but it doesn't have the black head-band. Often confused with the Common (or Indian) Myna, although that species is mainly brown and ground-dwelling, while the Noisy is grey and mainly found in trees.
Ecology: One of the most abundant urban birds, benefitting greatly from the planting of nectar-bearing plants. Social and gregarious, colonies (of up to 100) cooperate to drive other species out of their territories. As well as nectar, consumes insects, especially lerps, occasionally foraging on the ground.
Breeding: One of the most well-studied species of the many cooperative breeders in Australia and the first to be investigated in great detail.
Interactions with people: Becomes very tame, but will swoop people walking near nests.

DID YOU KNOW?

One of the unfortunate consequences of the presence of Noisy Miners is that they cannot stand any smaller (and lots of larger) species in the same area, and you end up with a much lower diversity of birds.

Bell Miner

Manorina melanophrys
Family: Meliphagidae:
Honeyeaters, Miners, Wattlebirds
and Friarbirds

Source of that delightful
incessant tinkling from the
tree-tops.

SIZE:

DISTRIBUTION:

HOME:

FOOD:

ACTIVE ZONE:

Identification: Extremely gregarious stoutly-built honeyeater. Plain olive-green plumage, slightly darker above. Sharp short yellow bill. Most conspicuous feature is the endlessly repeated single high-pitched bell-like note – *ping, ping, ping* – given by the birds in a large colony. Sexes indistinguishable.
Similar species: The tinkling bell call is *the* give-away; no other miner is olive.
Ecology: Forms large colonies of up to 200, which occupy a small area of tall eucalypt forest. Forages systematically through the foliage for insects, but is especially fond of the honeydew produced by lerps. Extremely aggressive towards most other birds.
Breeding: Breeds colonially and cooperatively with previous hatchings remaining in the group.
Interactions with people: Usually regarded positively, although the incessant calls can be exasperating for (some intolerant) picnickers.

DID YOU KNOW?

Bell Miners' addiction to honeydew has led them to protect the insects that produce it, driving away insectivorous birds that would otherwise consume the lerps. This can result in severe impacts on the trees within the colony.

Western Wattlebird

Anthochaera lunulata
Family: Meliphagidae:
Honeyeaters, Miners, Wattlebirds
and Friarbirds

A pugnacious autocratic extravert. Name refers to its neck
appendage, not the flowers.

SIZE:

DISTRIBUTION:

HOME:

FOOD:

ACTIVE ZONE:

Identification: Big and bold, this restless, ruthless honeyeater is well camouflaged, but draws attention by its aggressive behaviour and loud calls. Generally mottled dark brown with streaking all over. Notably, a wattlebird without wattles.

Similar species: Wattlebirds are all large, elongated and heavily built, bigger than most other honeyeaters. All wattlebirds have dark plumage, streaked with brown and white especially on the head and belly. Only found in Western Australia, so only likely confusion would be with the Red Wattlebird, which is much larger, has conspicuous red wattles and a black rather than dark brown crown.

Ecology: This nectar fanatic is fiercely protective of a good patch of flowering blossoms. Also eats insects and spiders, either gleaned from foliage or snatched from the air. Highly mobile, often chasing the waves of flowering trees. Always seems to be calling with strident *chok chock* followed by long cackles.

Breeding: Makes compact nests hidden deep within dense foliage. Extremely territorial when breeding.

Interactions with people: Seems oblivious to people.

DID YOU KNOW?

The numbers of this species have greatly increased in urban areas due to the abundance of nectar-bearing plants.

Little Wattlebird

Anthochaera chrysoptera
Family: Meliphagidae:
Honeyeaters, Miners, Wattlebirds
and Friarbirds

Slightly smaller than other
wattlebirds, but just as
aggressive and pugnacious.

SIZE:

DISTRIBUTION:

HOME:

FOOD:

ACTIVE ZONE:

Identification: The smallest of the wattlebirds and friarbirds, but no less feisty. This is the eastern version of the Western Wattlebird, with very similar plumage, but greyer beneath and clearer streaking. Does not have wattles.

Similar species: Could be confused with the Red Wattlebird, but is much smaller and lacks wattles. Similar to the Little Friarbird that shares many of its habits and habitats, but is darker and has a fully feathered head. Call is distinctive: a loud, raucous *cook-carock-carock* produced almost continuously.

Ecology: Nectar-driven and aggressively protects a rich foraging site. Also consumes any invertebrates encountered, gleaned from leaves or hawked in the air. Highly nomadic, following flowering. Moves about in dysfunctional (so it seems) family groups, endlessly bickering and chasing one another.

Breeding: Their nests, neat cups of shredded bark and grass, are well hidden within dense vegetation. Extremely territorial protectors of breeding sites.

Interactions with people: Too preoccupied with competitors to worry about mere humans.

DID YOU KNOW?

All wattlebirds possess long bristly tongues adapted to extracting nectar from flowers.

Red Wattlebird

Anthochaera carunculata
Family: Meliphagidae:
Honeyeaters, Miners, Wattlebirds
and Friarbirds

This familiar and assertive
bully produces one of the
characteristic sounds of
the bush.

SIZE:

DISTRIBUTION:

HOME:

FOOD:

ACTIVE ZONE:

Identification: Extremely conspicuous through its boisterous behaviour and raucous calling. Large, with dark streaked plumage, red eye and lighter coloured underside and distinctive yellow belly. Diagnostic red fleshy wattle is usually clearly detected, especially when the bird is perched openly and loudly vocalising.

Similar species: Being large, elongated and heavily built, it's bigger than most other honeyeaters, but could be confused with friarbirds that share many of its habits and habitats. Unlike the friarbirds, the Red has a fully feathered head and, of course, wattles.

Ecology: Nectar obsessed, it spends much of its time attempting to keep other honeyeaters away from its stash. Also eats insects and spiders, gleaned from foliage or snatched from the air. Constant and strident explosive *kwock* and *yack-a-yack* calls. Typically seen in small mobile flocks, endlessly bickering and chasing one another.

Breeding: Makes compact nests of bark, grasses and thin leaves, usually high above the ground.

Interactions with people: Has been greatly advantaged by the many nectar-producing plants now found in parks and gardens. Largely oblivious to people.

DID YOU KNOW?

The strange pendulous fleshy wattles in Red and Yellow Wattlebirds may be involved in mate choice or temperature regulation.

Yellow Wattlebird

Anthochaera paradoxa
Family: Meliphagidae:
Honeyeaters, Miners, Wattlebirds
and Friarbirds

Huge and aggressive, with
magnificent dangling wattles.

SIZE:

DISTRIBUTION:

HOME:

FOOD:

ACTIVE ZONE:

Identification: Enormous and unmistakable, this largest of all honeyeaters has the longest tail and obvious yellow wattles.
Similar species: Found only in Tasmania. With the only other large honeyeater there being the Little Wattlebird, identification is not likely to be an issue.
Ecology: This nectar fanatic is fiercely protective of a good patch of flowering blossoms. Opportunistically consumes fruit, invertebrates and insects, often snatching these from the air. Like all wattlebirds it calls often, vigorously facing the sky, using a remarkable variety of guttural clucks, gurgles and cackles.
Breeding: The nest is constructed solely by the female (the male is too busy chasing other birds away).
Interactions with people: Seems oblivious to people.

DID YOU KNOW?

The Yellow Wattlebird is both the largest honeyeater and the largest insectivorous bird in the world.

Helmeted Friarbird

Philemon buceroides
Family: Meliphagidae:
Honeyeaters, Miners, Wattlebirds
and Friarbirds

A raucous despot defiantly proclaiming with a harsh guttural call.

SIZE:

DISTRIBUTION:

HOME:

FOOD:

ACTIVE ZONE:

Identification: Large assertive honeyeater with a distinctive almost cylindrical bump (casque) on the top of its long black bill. Bare black facial skin extends well past the eye and is rounded in shape.

Similar species: Friarbirds are large honeyeaters with large wedge-shaped bills and heads usually covered in bare black skin. Most are grey above, buff below, but can be readily distinguished by the shape of the casque on the top of the bill. Sexes are identical. For the Helmeted, the cylindrical casque and rounded back of the facial skin are diagnostic.

Ecology: Occupies the same ecological niche as the wattlebirds, with which they are often seen, competing for the same blossoms. This friarbird consumes a much wider diet, including nectar, fruit, invertebrates and occasionally eggs and nestlings of small birds. Noisy, restless and aggressive, it continuously chases away other birds from contested foraging places.

Breeding: Builds a neat nest of grass and fine twigs well hidden in dense foliage. Breeding season appears to be influenced by seasonal flowering patterns.

Interactions with people: Has prospered due to all the nectar-bearing plants now found in parks and gardens. Can be approached when preoccupied with foraging.

DID YOU KNOW?

Named because of its bald head and sombre colours, reminiscent of friars.

Silver-crowned Friarbird

Philemon argenticeps
Family: Meliphagidae: Honeyeaters, Miners, Wattlebirds and Friarbirds

Loud and obnoxious, an extravert of tropical forests and gardens.

SIZE:

DISTRIBUTION:

HOME:

FOOD:

ACTIVE ZONE:

Identification: Typical friarbird in looks, but slender and elongated, with distinctive semi-circular large casque at the base of the bill. Bare black skin forms an angular triangle behind the ear. Crown is pale grey/silver, but is not especially prominent.

Similar species: Friarbirds are all similar, but readily distinguished by the shape of the casque. This is prominent and rounded in the Silver-crown in the Top End.

Ecology: Does the same ecological job as the wattlebirds found in southern parts of the country. Similarly preoccupied with obtaining nectar, but also consumes fruit, invertebrates and occasionally eggs and nestlings. Noisy, restless and aggressive, continuously chasing others from favourite foraging places. Fairly nomadic, responds to the rainfall patterns of the tropics.

Breeding: Builds a neat cup nest of grass and bark, suspended between fine branches.

Interactions with people: Its calls are loud and harsh, squawking and garbled, almost-human in tone. One of the commonest calls sounds like *more tabacco ay*, given only by the male.

DID YOU KNOW?

Many First Nations peoples believe the bizarre cackling noises produced by this bird mean it is swearing or exclaiming in the local language. They certainly do go on!

Helmeted Friarbird showing
its large casque

Noisy Friarbird

Philemon corniculatus
Family: Meliphagidae:
Honeyeaters, Miners, Wattlebirds
and Friarbirds

Familiar and fearless fanatics,
producing weird garbled
messages to a confused nation.

SIZE:

DISTRIBUTION:

HOME:

FOOD:

ACTIVE ZONE:

Identification: Busy and assertive, constantly chasing other birds of all species, pausing only to broadcast a bizarre cacophony of strange, harsh, prolonged and complex vocalisations, often including the well-known *four o'clock chock chock* call. A sharp triangular casque.
Similar species: All friarbirds are similar, but this is the only one with an entire head of bare black skin. Sexes are identical.
Ecology: Found in a large variety of wooded landscapes and especially in the eucalypts lining watercourses. A frequent visitor to backyards and gardens. A nectar fanatic, but also consumes fruit, invertebrates and occasionally eggs and nestlings. Noisy, restless and aggressive, forever chasing other birds from contested foraging places.
Breeding: Constructs a neat cup nest of grass and fine bark hanging from thin branches. Often highly protective of the nest site and will swoop people who get too close.
Interactions with people: Sometimes raids orchards and vineyards, bringing it into conflict with farmers.

DID YOU KNOW?

Most Noisy Friarbirds in southern Australia migrate north during the colder months, announcing their passage in their usual fashion: noisily!

Little Friarbird

Philemon citreogularis
Family: Meliphagidae:
Honeyeaters, Miners, Wattlebirds
and Friarbirds

The smaller friarbird, but still belligerent and noisy.

SIZE:

DISTRIBUTION:

HOME:

FOOD:

ACTIVE ZONE:

Identification: This is the smallest friarbird, with bare blue-black skin limited to a triangle beneath the eye. Produces a wide variety of pleasant and unpleasant noises, including the *chee-wip* song and a constant stream of raucous *rackety crookshank* calls.
Similar species: ID is easy, it's the only friarbird with no casque on the bill.
Ecology: Nectar obsessed, but also consumes flowers, seeds, fruit and a range of invertebrates. Noisy, restless and aggressive, continuously chasing other birds from contested foraging places.
Breeding: Builds a neat nest of grass and fine bark well hidden in dense foliage. Breeding season appears to be influenced by seasonal flowering patterns.
Interactions with people: Largely ignores people, though it will visit their gardens and bird feeders.

DID YOU KNOW?

Frequently the victim of the migratory cuckoo, the Eastern Koel. Like most cuckoos, the newly hatched baby Koel heaves any eggs or nestlings in the nest over the side. The host parents – in this case, Little Friarbirds – don't intervene even if they are present to watch.

Black-faced Cuckoo-shrike

Coracina novaehollandiae
Family: Campephagidae:
Cuckoo-shrikes

Ubiquitous and familiar,
its liquid trill and repetitive
wing shuffling can be seen
everywhere.

SIZE:

DISTRIBUTION:

HOME:

FOOD:

ACTIVE ZONE:

Identification: The most urban of the four cuckoo-shrikes. Well-known for its wing-shuffling on landing and lovely complex melodious trill. Pale grey, almost bluish plumage and full, entirely black face are diagnostic. Has a distinctive undulating flight. Sexes identical. The awkward common name is based on the cuckoo-like plumage and shrike-like bill (often shortened to 'Bifcus').
Similar species: Could be confused with the non-urban White-bellied Cuckoo-shrike, but that bird has either an entire black hood or almost no black on the face.
Ecology: Widespread, found in almost all habitats except dense forests and treeless deserts. Usually seen singly or in pairs, sallying out from a perch to snatch insects, but sometimes chasing prey to the ground or within foliage. In the cold months, may congregate in large flocks when migrating north.
Breeding: Both partners assist in building a small nest of grass and twigs placed on a horizontal branch.
Interactions with people: Very little interest in humans.

DID YOU KNOW?

Sometimes goes by the name 'Shufflewing' because of its weird habit of shuffling its wings when it lands.

White-breasted Woodswallow

Artamus leucorynchus
Family: Artamidae: Woodswallows and Butcherbirds

A delightful soaring insectivore, confidently swooping over a lake, parkland or streets.

SIZE:

DISTRIBUTION:

HOME:

FOOD:

ACTIVE ZONE:

Identification: Distinctive. The largest woodswallow and the most urban. Lovely slaty blue-grey above and linen-white beneath. Usually seen on the wing in flocks of a few to dozens or perched in tight huddles along a branch or on wires.

Similar species: Could be confused with the Masked Woodswallow, which is pale grey beneath and has a conspicuous black mask, but is much less likely to venture into towns.

Ecology: Abundant throughout much of the continent in all sorts of wooded habitat, but equally at home in the suburbs. An accomplished aerial forager, spending hours on the wing hunting insects, swooping gracefully and returning to a high perch. Will also take invertebrates from tree trunks and the foliage.

Breeding: Nests are delicate bowls of small twigs llined with grass, placed in forks of trees and sometimes on stumps. Breeds cooperatively with young from earlier broods assisting in the child care.

Interactions with people: Largely oblivious.

DID YOU KNOW?
The White-breasted is the most urban-adapted of all the wood-swallows, often seen perched on lines at busy intersections and swooping out to catch insects over crowded carparks.

Pied Currawong

Strepera graculina
Family: Artamidae:
Woodswallows, Butcherbirds
and Currawongs

Secretive, intelligent and
always up to something sinister.

SIZE:

DISTRIBUTION:

HOME:

FOOD:

ACTIVE ZONE:

Identification: Large, elongated and alert. Seems to be entirely black, but the prominent white wing patch is revealed when flying. Bright, alert and unsettling yellow eyes. Well known for the familiar loud ringing *clonk, clonk* call.

Similar species: Easily confused with the Grey Currawong, but has darker plumage and bill shape (curved upper edge in Pied, straight in Grey), but best distinguished by the call (Pied goes *clonk*, Grey goes *clink*). Greys tend to avoid towns.

Ecology: Abundant and familiar throughout eastern Australia, but historically found mainly at higher altitudes. Lives in most treed habitats, but has prospered in towns and cities everywhere. The traditional winter altitudinal migration down to the lowlands in some areas has led to its permanent presence in lower altitudes.

Breeding: Breeds mainly in spring, constructing large stick nests placed very high up in a tall tree.

Interactions with people: Although they have lost all fear of humans, are still wary, even when scavenging scraps.

DID YOU KNOW?

Historically regarded as a nestling predator, its impact was minimised by being absent during the breeding season in lowland areas. Recently, however, many Currawongs have remained in the lower altitudes throughout the year, causing serious loses for small birds.

Pied Butcherbird

Cracticus nigrogularis
Family: Artamidae:
Woodswallows and Butcherbirds

Smart, predatory and observant. Expert aerial acrobats, some with gorgeous melodic songs.

SIZE:

DISTRIBUTION:

HOME:

FOOD:

ACTIVE ZONE:

Identification: Medium-sized, black and white with a distinctive black 'executioner's hood' covering the entire head down to the chest. Grey bill has a sinister hook. Sexes indistinguishable.

Similar species: Butcherbirds are stouter and smaller than currawongs and the Magpie, and have a distinctive hook on the end of the bill. Only potential confusion here would be with the Grey Currawong, which wears a black helmet and has a dark grey back.

Ecology: A vigilant hunter with extraordinary eyesight, spying skinks and grasshoppers far below or taking moths and dragonflies on the wing. Can be seen alone, in pairs or small family groups. Extremely vocal, producing pure flute-like notes in melodious choruses, often delivered by multiple birds. Pairs frequently duet.

Breeding: Typically breeds in spring, sometimes cooperatively. Builds large stick nests high in eucalypts.

Interactions with people: The urban butcherbird becomes entirely fearless and is adept at training humans to offer it morsels. Can become aggressive towards humans coming too close to nests, *à la* the Magpie.

DID YOU KNOW?

The song of the Pied is one of the most beautiful bird vocalisations anywhere, with soaring melodies and pure flute-like notes. These songs are learned by listening and extensive practising and young males can often be heard rehearsing quietly when they think they are alone.

Grey Butcherbird

Cracticus torquatus
Family: Artamidae:
Woodswallows and Butcherbirds

Intelligent, confident, brilliant
in the air and not afraid to
sing in public.

SIZE:

DISTRIBUTION:

HOME:

FOOD:

ACTIVE ZONE:

Identification: Somewhat smaller than a Magpie, with a stouter stance and defiant air. Wears a distinctive black 'cyclist's helmet' with a prominent white collar extending almost all the way to the back. The back is dark ashy grey rather than black. Bill is grey with black hooked end. Sexes similar, but female has a large white lore.
Similar species: Main potential for confusion here is with the Pied Currawong which has extensive black hood reaching to the lower breast. Pieds and Greys often hang out together, when they become a bit easier to distinguish.
Ecology: Usually seen in pairs or small family groups. Prefers more open wooded habitats so the suburbs are ideal. Extremely acrobatic in the air, snatching insects on the wing, but also adept at pouncing to the ground and gleaning among the foliage. Highly vocal, with complex loud calls given by the whole group. Notes can be musical as well as harsh.
Breeding: Typically breeds in spring, usually as part of a cooperative group. Constructs large stick nests high up with a good view.
Interactions with people: Has no fear of humans and is a regular visitor to bird tables and verandah railings where it waits for bits of cheese to be tossed. It never misses!

DID YOU KNOW?
The remarkably complex songs are unique to each family group and can differ significantly over short distances.

Black Butcherbird

Cracticus quoyi
Family: Artamidae:
Woodswallows and Butcherbirds

Tropical, secretive and somewhat elusive, typically staying out of view.

SIZE:

DISTRIBUTION:

HOME:

FOOD:

ACTIVE ZONE:

Identification: The largest of the typical butcherbirds (the Magpie being atypical), but often hard to spot as it hides in dense vegetation most of the time. The only entirely black butcherbird. Sexes indistinguishable.

Similar species: No issues with identifying this bird as a butchie, but could be confused with several all-black birds in the tropical rainforest. These include the Spangled Drongo (though its fish-tail is a give-away) and the male Eastern Koel (but the calls will sort them out quickly).

Ecology: Usually seen singly or in a pair. Mainly found in densely wooded habitats such as rainforests and mangroves, but does visit gardens and parks if there is plenty of cover. Eats a wide variety of prey, usually by gleaning among the foliage or pouncing on the ground. Calls are loud and varied, deeper than other butcherbirds.

Breeding: Nests are well hidden, high in the densest thickets. Can be very assertive near the nest, driving other birds away.

Interactions with people: The introvert among butcherbirds, shy and retiring though some individuals can become slightly tame.

DID YOU KNOW?

Butcherbirds get their name from their habit of storing prey in 'larders', usually a branch with plenty of sharp protruding sticks. The foodstuffs – small mammals, lizards, baby birds – are spiked there for later consumption.

Male Australian Magpie pauses while foraging for worms

Australian Magpie

Cracticus tibicen
Family: Artamidae:
Woodswallows and Butcherbirds

Iconic, idolised, feared and fed:
Australia's favourite bird and
the most vicious.

SIZE:

DISTRIBUTION:

HOME:

FOOD:

ACTIVE ZONE:

Identification: Possibly the most familiar bird in the country. Boldly black and white with the pattern varying greatly with geography. The male has a sharp edge to its white neck, whereas this transitions gradually in females. Usually seen foraging on lawns.

Similar species: Possibly confused with the Pied Currawong or other butcherbirds, but is larger and plumper than both and has white on its head.

Ecology: One of our most common and widespread birds, found in any open treed habitat, but most abundant in urban areas. Maintains and defends year-round territories. Pairs often remain on the same patch for many years. Specialised at foraging for below-ground worms and grubs, which it locates by listening.

Breeding: Breeds in spring, otherwise known as 'Magpie Season'. Territorial behaviour peaks prior to egg laying and ceases when the nestlings fledge.

Interactions with people: Some males are infamous for swooping people coming too close to the nest when nestlings are present. Yet also beloved by many who feed them and form close relationships.

DID YOU KNOW?

According to one creation story from the Whadjuk Nyoongar people around Perth, Magpies were responsible for separating the earth from the sky, leading to the first sunrise, something they continue to celebrate every morning with their glorious song.

White-winged Chough

Corcorax melanorhamphos
Family: Corcoracidae: Australian Mudnesters (Choughs)

Strange yet beguiling, perpetually squabbling families wandering, oblivious.

SIZE:

DISTRIBUTION:

HOME:

FOOD:

ACTIVE ZONE:

Identification: A large, ground-foraging Magpie-like bird, always in noisy conspicuous family groups. Matt black plumage with a long murderous-looking bill and disturbingly blood-red eyes. Appears all black until it flies, when the prominent white flight feathers are visible. Sexes are indistinguishable. Although it closely resembles European Choughs (hence the name), they are not closely related.

Similar species: A casual look might confuse it with a Magpie or Pied Currawong, but the Chough has no visible white part while on the ground.

Ecology: A strange bird, with complex behaviours and a quirky personality; always looks like it is plotting something. Typically found in family groups, which may number five to about 20. Forages by systematically working over a patch of woodland leaf litter, probing for insects, worms, seeds and plant bulbs.

Breeding: All group members (not always usefully) are involved in constructing the large bowl-shaped mud nest and assist in raising the young.

Interactions with people: Although it has successfully moved into towns, it is too preoccupied with its own issues to notice people.

DID YOU KNOW?

Will kidnap juveniles from neighbouring groups if it needs additional members.

Australian Raven

Corvus coronoides
Family: Corvidae: Crows and Ravens

Revered and reviled, risk averse, resourceful and remarkably smart.

SIZE:

DISTRIBUTION:

HOME:

FOOD:

ACTIVE ZONE:

Identification: Large, robust and imposing. Always alert and on the lookout. Typical corvid looks – glossy blue-black plumage in sunlight – but has distinctively long and conspicuous throat hackles, clearly visible when calling. As with all corvids, the best identification is its call: high-pitched and drawn-out loud cry of *waaaa-aaaah-aaaahk*, ending in low, slow 'death rattle'.

Similar species: There are five Australian corvids. All are shiny jet-black with large dark bills. Three species are found in cities. The Australian Raven is the main species found in Sydney and Perth. Its neck hackles and long call are diagnostic.

Ecology: Found across the continent in all habitats, it has moved into cities only in recent decades. Uses its exceptional intelligence to exploit every aspect of the urban landscape, finding places to obtain all sorts of food, safe nest sites and activities to pass the time.

Breeding: Monogamous and territorial. Pairs construct large stick nests high in trees.

Interactions with people: Always wary, but can become slightly more confiding in urban areas. Adept at scavenging without being noticed.

DID YOU KNOW?

The incredibly intelligent Australian Raven is notable – along with other corvids – for its use of tools; it has been known to use fence posts to bash snails against before eating them.

Little Raven

Corvus mellori
Family: Corvidae: Crows
and Ravens

Observant and clever,
always seems to be
plotting something.

SIZE:

DISTRIBUTION:

HOME:

FOOD:

ACTIVE ZONE:

Identification: Somewhat smaller corvid with shorter spikier throat hackles and the habit of flicking its wings when calling. Flies with a direct but jerky wing beat. Typical call consists of short guttural *ark-ark-aaark*, which ends abruptly.

Similar species: Though all five native corvids look extremely similar the Little Raven is the common corvid in Melbourne. Spiky hackles and clipped abrupt calls are distinctive.

Ecology: Resourceful but risk averse, it's still able to exploit the many opportunities available in urban areas. Performs an important service of cleaning up discarded edible wastes and road kill.

Breeding: Breeds semi-cooperatively, with pairs building nests in neighbouring trees, although the nests themselves are guarded. Sometimes nests close to Australian Ravens.

Interactions with people: Rarely approachable, but will discreetly raid pet food and discarded lunches in parks and schoolyards.

DID YOU KNOW?

The Little Raven was only 'discovered' during the 1960s, when researchers realised that the smaller birds often accompanying Australian Ravens in the inland were actually a different species.

Torresian Crow

Corvus orru
Family: Corvidae: Crows
and Ravens

The tropical crow of Australia,
famous for learning how to
safely consume cane toads.

SIZE:

DISTRIBUTION:

HOME:

FOOD:

ACTIVE ZONE:

Identification: Large, glossy, slim and attentive. Most distinctive features are the nasal staccato calls – *ok-ok-ok* – finishing abruptly, the very short throat hackles and conspicuous wing flicking when calling or upon landing.

Similar species: The only corvid of the tropical north and the only one to be seen in towns within its distribution.

Ecology: Uses its exceptional intelligence to exploit every aspect of the urban landscape, finding places to obtain almost any food, nest safely and observe us closely. Social, noisy and always seemingly up to something. Torresians often form large communal roosts in cities, apparently as a way of efficiently finding food.

Breeding: Monogamous and fairly sedentary, at least in cities. Pairs construct large stick nests high in trees and tall structures such as telecommunication towers, although some populations of Torresians have started nesting on inner-city buildings.

Interactions with people: Never tame or confiding but will – discreetly – steal pet food and visit bird feeders. Infamous for unzipping school lunchboxes, stealing windscreen wipers and removing the rubber seals from car windows. Malicious or just curious?

DID YOU KNOW?

Their distinctive call may sound repetitive and unpleasant, but has been shown to be one of the most complex of all birdsongs, and can be regarded as genuine language.

Satin Bowerbird

Ptilonorhynchus violaceus
Family: Ptilonorhynchidae:
Bowerbirds

Spectacular and remarkable
bird found building its bower
in suburban gardens.

SIZE:

DISTRIBUTION:

HOME:

FOOD:

ACTIVE ZONE:

Identification: Large, chunky bowerbird with powerful bill and violet eyes. The mature male is a gleaming deep royal blue, though may look simply black in the shade. The female and younger male are mossy green above with brown wings and tail, and speckled belly. The male slowly develops its full blue plumage over six years, with an untidy patchwork of blue and green in the later years.

Similar species: A male could be confused with an Asian Koel or a Spangled Drongo, but is far stockier and those species are rarely seen on the ground.

Ecology: Mainly found in rainforest and dense moist eucalypt forest, but can be quite abundant where houseyards and parks are adjacent to forests. Forages for fruit and insects in leaf litter and sometimes in foliage.

Breeding: Like all bowerbirds, the male is utterly preoccupied with its bower while the female nests and raises the chicks unaided. The male decorates bowers with mainly dark blue objects used to attract females.

Interactions with people: Traditionally, the blue decorations were short-lived fruits, flowers and feathers, but now plastic straws, pegs and bottle tops are commonly used, and can last forever.

DID YOU KNOW?

Bowers are orientated very carefully so that the sunlight illuminates the bird's display and plumage.

Great Bowerbird

Chlamydera nuchalis
Family: Ptilonorhynchidae:
Bowerbirds

A surprising and entertaining inhabitant of many a tropical garden.

SIZE:

DISTRIBUTION:

HOME:

FOOD:

ACTIVE ZONE:

Identification: Large, robust bowerbird with long legs and clear, clean grey plumage. Apart from light cross-hatching on wings and a tiny pink crest (usually not visible), its plain appearance is diagnostic. Female very similar.

Similar species: Some overlap with the distribution of the Spotted Bowerbird in central Queensland, but that species is smaller and browner, and rarely enter towns.

Ecology: For lucky people in the tropics, having two species of these extraordinary birds, Satin and Great, building their bowers, complete with all the decorations and bizarre behaviours in ordinary backyards is simply amazing! Greats collect objects of three colours: whitish bones and snail shells, green fruit and leaves, and just a few red items (often plastic).

Breeding: Like all bowerbirds, the male cares little for anything apart from its bower while the female nests separately and raises the chicks alone.

Interactions with people: The bird steals any items of the correct colour it can carry to add to its bower decorations.

DID YOU KNOW?

The only bowerbird in which several young males work together to practise their bower construction and decorating skills prior to competing with older males for the attention of females. This apprenticeship can last for seven years.

Australasian Figbird

Specotheres vieilloti
Family: Oriolidae: Figbirds and Orioles

Gregarious and noisy, a glaring red-eyed fig addict.

SIZE:

DISTRIBUTION:

HOME:

FOOD:

ACTIVE ZONE:

Identification: Medium-sized, dumpy bird with olive back and black tail. The male has a distinctive red mask around the eyes, which becomes very bright during the breeding season. Bill is dark. The female has strong vertical streaking down its off-white front. Always seen in close flocks of 10–40, either well hidden in the dense canopy or perched conspicuously on lines near a fruiting tree.

Similar species: The male is obvious; the female could easily be confused with an Olive-backed Oriole, but she doesn't have that species' red bill.

Ecology: Exceptionally gregarious, forming large boisterous flocks that assertively occupy a fruiting tree. Calls incessantly, the most common being a loud sharp *twoo-twoo* or *too-weer, tower*. Found in all habitats with fruiting trees, but has successfully colonised urban areas wherever figs (especially the Moreton Bay) are present. Continues to expand its distribution south, having recently crossed into Victoria from the north.

Breeding: Breeds in loose colonies, with numerous flimsy nests being located within a single large fig tree.

Interactions with people: Visits backyards with fruit trees and sometimes takes fruit such as blueberries from bird feeders.

DID YOU KNOW?

The Australian Figbird is a favourite foster parent for the migratory cuckoo, the Eastern Koel.

Olive-backed Oriole

Oriolus sagittatus
Family: Oriolidae: Figbirds and Orioles

Superb songster, decorating the morning with lovely flutey calls.

SIZE:

DISTRIBUTION:

HOME:

FOOD:

ACTIVE ZONE:

Identification: Olive-green above with pale front thickly streaked with black slashes. The male is significantly brighter in colour and has a red bill. Mainly found alone or in pairs; rarely in large flocks. Call is the most conspicuous feature, the most often heard a lovely liquid, rolling *olli-ollill-ollilly*.

Similar species: Very similar to the adult female Australasian Figbird, but is brighter green and has an orange-pink rather than a grey bill. The Oriole has bright red eyes, while the Figbird has red skin surrounding its black eyes.

Ecology: Retiring and often hard to see within the dense canopy, but is always calling. Forages for fruit and berries, but will take any insects encountered.

Breeding: Breeds mainly during the wet season in the tropics and late spring to early summer further south.

Interactions with people: Although abundant in urban areas has not become tame.

DID YOU KNOW?

As well as a range of sweet clear calls, this oriole makes strange rasping and squawking sounds. A brilliant ventriloquist and a mimic of other birds.

163

Spangled Drongo

Dicrurus bracteatus
Family: Dicruridae: Drongos

A restless, energetic and comical sprite producing endless strange un-birdlike noises.

SIZE:

DISTRIBUTION:

HOME:

FOOD:

ACTIVE ZONE:

Identification: Glossy black plumage, with tints of iridescent green and purple in sunshine with a distinctive flared forked fish-tail. Continuously performing contorted flights while broadcasting an astonishing array of weird electronic sounds: harsh, grating and sometimes otherworldly.

Similar species: Although the forked tail is diagnostic, could be confused with a male Eastern Koel. Wait a few moments, however, and listen for the bizarre noises; a dead give-away!

Ecology: Likes the edges of denser forests and woodlands, but happy to visit urban parks and backyards. Brilliant aerial predator of insects, but has a broad, indeed alarming, diet which includes nestlings, geckoes, and even small birds consumed whole. Always restless, perched high on an exposed branch, calling and sallying out to snatch flying insects.

Breeding: Intolerant of other species near their nests.

Interactions with people: Can become extremely tame when residing near people and enjoys grabbing food items tossed into the air.

DID YOU KNOW?

'Spangled' refers to the sequin-like colours that can be seen in bright light, while 'drongo' is the traditional name for the bird in Madagascar. The connotation of stupidity came later and was associated with a racehorse of that name that never won, and the people who kept betting on it.

The ever-alert
and active
Spangled Drongo

Magpie-lark

Grallina cyanoleuca
Family: Monarchidae: Monarchs
(Magpie-larks)

The bold black-and-white
'Pee-Wee' or 'Mud-Lark'
of every park and garden
in the country.

SIZE:

DISTRIBUTION:

HOME:

FOOD:

ACTIVE ZONE:

Identification: Unmistakable, striding confidently across the lawn or fossicking in the muddy edge of a pond. Striking black and white patchwork with convenient features allowing easy sexing: the male has a thin horizontal line crossing the eye while the female has a thick black stripe running vertically through the eye. Strident, ear-piercing *peewee-peewee* or even louder alarm *peet-peet* are diagnostic.

Similar species: There are plenty of other black and white birds out there, but none look or sound like the 'Pee-Wee'.

Ecology: One of the most abundant and widespread birds in the country, found in all habitats, but none more so than urban areas. Has taken full advantage of all the watered lawns and mown fields, as well as the ponds it likes to breed near.

Breeding: Builds a remarkable circular mud nest reinforced with grass and placed conspicuously on a large horizontal branch, often above or near water.

Interactions with people: Fearless, especially if you approach a nest with chicks too closely. Can spend considerable time beating up its reflection in hubcaps, wing mirrors and reflecting windows.

DID YOU KNOW?

The Magpie-lark has a loud and effective system of vocal communication both between mated partners and neighbouring pairs, often involving intricate duetting.

Grey Fantail

Rhipidura albiscapa
Family: Rhipiduridae: Fantails

Energetic, restless and talkative, flitting erratically about the foliage chasing insects.

SIZE:

DISTRIBUTION:

HOME:

FOOD:

ACTIVE ZONE:

Identification: Fairly distinctive, a hyperactive though rather dull-coloured fantail, constantly moving from branch to branch, fanning its tail and twisting around. Grey above and off-white below.

Similar species: The only similar species are found in northern coastal areas and are almost never seen in towns.

Ecology: A busy and clever insectivore, perpetually in motion searching for insects in the foliage or the air. The constant tail-fanning frightens insects into flight where they are deftly snatched. Found everywhere across the continent. Produces a variety of chittering, chattering sounds. Abundant and well known.

Breeding: Constructs a tidy 'wine-glass' nest with tapering 'stem' from grasses and cobwebs, positioned on a thin horizontal branch, often not far above the ground. Pair-bonded, but has a surprisingly high level of matings outside the pair bond.

Interactions with people: Tolerates people, but has no real interest.

DID YOU KNOW?

Mysteriously, this species often builds numerous nests during the breeding season, but only uses one. Maybe this is to confuse predators, but no one is certain.

Willie Wagtail

Rhipidura leucophrys
Family: Rhipiduridae: Fantails

Familiar, spirited and utterly
fearless, a much-loved sprite.

SIZE:

DISTRIBUTION:

HOME:

FOOD:

ACTIVE ZONE:

Identification: Unmistakable: black throat and upper breast, with white lower breast, belly and under tail. Distinctive black fantail, rocking left to right. One of the most popular and familiar birds in the country. Its name in many First Nations languages is clearly based on its call: djikirrigj-djikirridj in Kunwinjku (Arnhem Land) and tjintir-tjintir(*pa*) in Pitjantjatjara (Central Australia).
Similar species: Could be confused with the Restless Flycatcher, a similarly black and white flycatcher, but that species is much slimmer, sticks to the trees and rarely enters towns.
Ecology: Found almost everywhere in the country (a vagrant only occasionally makes it to Tassie), but avoids dense forests. An accomplished aerial acrobat, able to expertly pursue and snatch insects from the air. Has two well-known calls, the harsh *chiti-chiti-chiti* when agitated and the delightfully famous *sweet-pretty-creature*. On moonlit nights, this can go on ad nauseum.
Breeding: Builds a small perfect cup of very fine grasses and cobwebs secured to a horizontal branch, often not far above the ground.
Interactions with people: Fearless and confiding, one of the birds happy to live closely with people.

DID YOU KNOW?

Among the most commonly mentioned birds in First Nations stories, in which it is often know as 'the little messenger' who brings communications from the spirit world.

Rufous Whistler

Pachycephala rufiventris
Family: Pachycephalidae:
Whistlers

Common and familiar
throughout the continent, its
clear, ringing call is a part of
the Aussie bush.

SIZE:

DISTRIBUTION:

HOME:

FOOD:

ACTIVE ZONE:

Identification: The male is unmistakable: distinctive gorgeous white throat and rich orange-rufous underparts separated by a smart black band across the breast. Female is grey above with fine vertical dark dashes against light buff belly. Most conspicuous feature, however, is its signature call: the loud, penetrating *ee-chong!* heard in bushland everywhere. Unlike other whistlers, is (almost) never seen on the ground.

Similar species: Male is obvious, but the female looks similar to other whistlers (especially juveniles), which also have lightly streaked fronts. However, no other whistlers come into towns.

Ecology: Occurs in every wooded habitat on the continent, although it avoids the densest and wettest forests. An alert vigilant bird, often seen calling from a prominent branch before continuing its relentless foraging for insects among the foliage. Occasionally consumes fruits and seeds.

Breeding: Although the female alone builds the nest (the male is too busy singing), both partners share the incubation and child-care duties.

Interactions with people: No direct contact, but will visit houseyards on foraging trips.

DID YOU KNOW?

One of our best songsters, its distinctive call –
often triggered by sudden loud noises – has
given it the nickname 'Thunderbird'.

Olive-backed Sunbird

Cinnyris jugularis
Family: Nectariniidae: Sunbirds

Exquisite jewel, flitting rapidly about, often hovering hummingbird-style.

SIZE:

DISTRIBUTION:

HOME:

FOOD:

ACTIVE ZONE:

Identification: Tiny and unmistakable; the only sunbird in Australia. Olive-green back and bright yellow belly. The male has a shimmering royal blue bib (gorget), while the female is yellow all the way to the bill. Distinctive long curved bill.
Similar species: Nothing else remotely like it.
Ecology: A restless nectar addict, found in coastal forests as well as parks and gardens throughout the tropics. Pairs usually seen together, flitting busily from flower to flower. Call is a prolonged insect-like buzz, somewhat like the sound of foam rubbed on glass.
Breeding: Constructs a wondrous elongated hanging nest placed on outer branches often above water. In towns, will attach nests to eaves and sheltered structures, often near places used by people. Extremely territorial when breeding.
Interactions with people: Loses all fear of people when living within urban areas. Will partake of sugary fluids from bird feeders.

DID YOU KNOW?

Sunbirds are found from Africa to Asia. Of the approximately 145 species, only one has made it to Australia.

Mistletoebird

Dicaeum hirundinaceum
Family: Dicaeidae: Flowerpeckers
(Mistletoebirds)

A gorgeous busy little
bright red gem, obsessed
with mistletoe.

SIZE:

DISTRIBUTION:

HOME:

FOOD:

ACTIVE ZONE:

Identification: A small, stubby bird with the male mainly black and vivid scarlet while the female is dull brown. Both have a distinctive red-pink under-tail.
Similar species: The male could be mistaken for a Scarlet Honeyeater, but has a completely black head. The female could be confused with a large number of smaller brown species, but the red vent is diagnostic.
Ecology: Occurs wherever mistletoe, a parasite, grows on trees. A rare example of a bird utilising just one type of plant, and a plant that can't reproduce without the bird: classic mutualism. The bird will, however, sometimes consume nectar from other trees, and insects. The mistletoe fruit is adapted to passing through the digestive tract; the large seed retains its sticky coating. When defecating, the bird positions itself so that the seed attaches to a branch, thus ensuring that it can parasitise the tree.
Breeding: Breeding starts with the appearance of mistletoe berries, which can vary geographically. The pair may produce three broods per year if food is plentiful.
Interactions with people: None.

DID YOU KNOW?

The Mistletoebird spends a quarter of its day foraging in the summer and nearly a third in winter. Mistletoe fruit make up 85 per cent of its diet.

Red-whiskered Bulbul
with a freshly
caught dragonfly

Red-whiskered Bulbul

Pycnonotus jocosus
Family: Pycnonotidae: Bulbuls

Noisy, bold and assertive, an introduced species that has not moved far.

SIZE:

DISTRIBUTION:

HOME:

FOOD:

ACTIVE ZONE:

Identification: Distinctive and confident, a medium-sized pugnacious introduced species patchily distributed along the eastern seaboard. Most abundant in Sydney. Perches and calls conspicuously from exposed branches, launching to snatch insects from the air. Highly distinctive sharp black crest with tell-tale red and white patch on cheek and red under-tail.
Similar species: None.
Ecology: Bulbuls are a huge family of fruit-eating birds from all over Asia. In its native range, it resides in thickets beside rice fields and agricultural areas. Here, it has prospered in only a few areas, but remains a bird of dense low foliage. Sedentary and territorial, but joins large groups to roost. Calls are loud, pleasant and varied: commonly chattering and scolding.
Breeding: Vigorously defends relatively large areas around the nest during the breeding season.
Interactions with people: Tolerant, but mainly ignores them.

DID YOU KNOW?

A common cage bird in Asia, where its bright *kink-a-jou* calls are appreciated.

Silvereye

Zosterops lateralis
Family: Zosteropidae: White-eyes
(Silver-eyes)

Energetic and busy, deftly working its way through the foliage as part of a lively flock.

SIZE:

DISTRIBUTION:

HOME:

FOOD:

ACTIVE ZONE:

Identification: The common silvereye found in most of the cities of Australia. Lots of plumage variation, but all look like a small, slim, olive-green warbler with a prominent eye ring (like circular spectacles). Mostly grey underneath, but some have orangey sides. Sexes indistinguishable.

Similar species: The Yellow White-eye found in Darwin has a yellow breast and belly. Numerous small greenish honeyeaters might be confusing, but none of those have the conspicuous eye-ring.

Ecology: A busy gregarious forager of small insects and sugary juices obtained by piercing ripe fruits. Constantly moves through the canopy in loose groups. While in motion, it keeps in contact with others by calling continuously, a high-pitched *pseee*, *psee* and other musical trills.

Breeding: Usually breeds in spring or early summer, weaving a tiny, neat nest of fine grasses, thistledown, spiderwebs, moss and sometimes horse hair.

Interactions with people: Although it eats lots of harmful insects around orchards and vineyards, it is regarded as a significant pest in some areas because it spoils fruit, especially grapes, by piercing them for the juice.

DID YOU KNOW?

Vast numbers of the Tasmanian population cross Bass Strait every year to temporarily escape the cold winter, some dispersing as far as southern Queensland – an impressive undertaking for such a tiny bird.

Common Blackbird

Turdus merula
Family: Turdidae: Thrushes

Instantly recognisable from English children's books, alert, conspicuous and cocky.

SIZE:

DISTRIBUTION:

HOME:

FOOD:

ACTIVE ZONE:

Identification: Abundant in towns and cities throughout south-eastern Australia. Typically seen confidently hopping across the lawn, pausing to look around, before pouncing on a worm. The male is shiny black with a bright orange-yellow bill. The female is dark brown all over with faint streaks on front.

Similar species: The male is unmistakable. Around Melbourne (the site of the original release in 1856), the female could be mistaken for a Song Thrush, but the Blackbird is larger and doesn't have the thrush's clearly spotted front.

Ecology: An iconic bird of city parks and gardens around the world, now found throughout most of Victoria and New South Wales and continuing to expand into southern Queensland. Ground-foraging species that has benefitted greatly from well-watered lawns and rows of dense hedges. As well as worms and other invertebrates, also consumes fruit and berries. Sings its loud, pleasant variable songs almost continuously through winter and spring, starting well before dawn.

Breeding: Builds a neat mud nest lined with fine grasses, often placed in garden shrubs and trees as well as awnings and hanging plants.

Interactions with people: Mostly enjoyed, but is unpopular when it consumes strawberries, berries and stone fruit.

DID YOU KNOW?

Released in Australia to provide familiar sights and sounds from 'home' back in Europe.

Song Thrush

Turdus philomelos
Family: Turdidae: Thrushes

Rather nervous thrush, skulking unobtrusively in the shadows; has a fondness for snails.

SIZE:

DISTRIBUTION:

HOME:

FOOD:

ACTIVE ZONE:

Identification: An introduced, ground-dwelling, secretive thrush that hops into the open briefly before disappearing back into the undergrowth. Has a distinctive yellowish-off-white front covered in prominent dark-brown streaks. Upper parts are brown. Sexes identical.
Similar species: Only possible confusion (in poor light) could be with a female Common Blackbird, but the Song Thrush is larger and lacks the clear breast stripes.
Ecology: A denizen of dark places beneath hedges and undergrowth of suburban gardens and city parks around Melbourne. When it ventures out in search of worms, snails and fallen fruit, remains close to cover. Often has a favourite stone – an 'anvil' – on which snail shells are smashed open. Despite the name, is silent for most of the year, but does produce a delightful loud and prolonged song full of pleasant notes and meaningful pauses.
Breeding: The female builds a neat, round mud and grass nest lined with dry grass and feathers, similar to the Common Blackbird's nest.
Interactions with people: Welcomed because of its consumption of snails in private gardens and cheerful song.

DID YOU KNOW?

There are 175 species in the Family Turdidae, found almost everywhere on the planet, including the Song Thrush and Common Blackbird which were introduced in Australia in the 1850s.

Common Myna

Acridotheres tristis
Family: Sturnidae: Starlings and Mynas

Fearless, aggressive and belligerent, noisily squabbling and joining huge roosts at night.

SIZE:

DISTRIBUTION:

HOME:

FOOD:

ACTIVE ZONE:

Identification: Fairly distinctive with brown plumage and black head with vivid yellow bill, legs and eye-ring. Almost always seen in active, noisy groups on the ground.
Similar species: Often mistaken for the native Noisy Miner, though that species is much smaller and more slender, is usually seen in trees and is mostly grey. Both have yellow bills and patches behind the eyes, features less obvious in the Noisy Miner.
Ecology: Mainly insectivorous, but will consume almost anything. Highly social and very noisy, one of the most conspicuous birds in the downtown areas of many cities. At night, they gather to roost in sometimes enormous flocks, producing a deafening racket, often using building awnings, electrical structures and electronic billboards.
Breeding: Pairs occupy tree hollows, sometimes evicting other species, and have been known to kill nestlings and puncture eggs of other species. Competition for tree hollows is a serious conservation issue.
Interactions with people: One of the species that has exploited many parts of the human world, all while strutting about with a belligerent attitude.

DID YOU KNOW?

Mynas were intentionally brought to Australia to control insect pests and are now regarded as a major problem. One of three birds listed in the IUCN's list of '100 of the World's Worst Invasive Alien Species'. (The others are the Common Starling and a species of bulbul.)

Common Starling

Sturnus vulgaris
Family: Sturnidae: Starlings and Mynas

Active, gregarious and assertive, often foraging out of town, but returning to roost in the city.

SIZE:

DISTRIBUTION:

HOME:

FOOD:

ACTIVE ZONE:

Identification: Smallish, ground-foraging bird, superficially black, but heavily speckled with white arrows or metallic blue-black in good light. Distinctive flat head and sharp dagger-like bill. Always seen in groups and can form enormous flocks numbering in the thousands, which perform murmurations – spectacular displays of closely spaced birds wheeling and swirling in extraordinary patterns – when preparing to roost.

Similar species: Not many other birds look or behave like Common Starlings, although Common Mynas, much larger and brown, not black, come close.

Ecology: Can be extremely abundant in rural areas where huge flocks forage busily in the fields. Mainly consumes insects, but will opportunistically exploit almost anything edible.

Breeding: Builds large, untidy grass nests in roof cavities and tree hollows. One of the pair often seen perched at the entrance.

Interactions with people: The aerial murmurations are awe-inspiring, but the sheer quantity of droppings deposited on the ground (or parked vehicles) beneath the roost sites is much less welcome.

DID YOU KNOW?

Has a remarkably diverse suite of calls including melodious whistles, electronic buzzes and mimicry of many other species.

Double-barred Finch

Taeniopygia bichenovii
Family: Estrildidae: Finches and Mannikins

Lovely and heart-warming, busily fossicking for seeds in buzzing boisterous flocks.

SIZE:

DISTRIBUTION:

HOME:

FOOD:

ACTIVE ZONE:

Identification: Small and boldly striped. The two black bands across the white breast are diagnostic of the Double-barred Finch. Its dark back and heavily spotted wings are distinctive, but may only be visible through binoculars. Typically observed in ever-moving groups foraging efficiently along the ground.
Similar species: The two black breast bands are unique and no other finch is this white. Could be confused with a White-fronted Chat or Southern Whiteface, but these are never seen in urban areas.
Ecology: Found in treed habitats with plenty of understorey, including patches near the suburbs. Will venture into backyards if it can find suitable grasses or feeders with small seeds. Usually seen in flocks of 10–20, sometimes much larger. Call is a nasally double *teeat-teeat*, almost mournful in character.
Breeding: Breeds somewhat communally, with numerous nests built close together in low shrubs and lower branches.
Interactions with people: One of very few finches that will swarm to feeders if small seeds are offered.

DID YOU KNOW?
Sometimes known as the Owl Finch because of the round face mask.

Common Starling
feeding insects to
its chicks

Red-browed Finch

Neochmia temporalis
Family: Estrildidae: Finches and Mannikins

A delightful gem, flitting through the undergrowth beside bushland tracks.

SIZE:

DISTRIBUTION:

HOME:

FOOD:

ACTIVE ZONE:

Identification: Probably the most abundant finch found in urban areas (although the Double-barred Finch may disagree), but easy to miss because of its foliage-blending olive-green and grey plumage. The distinctive bright red face mask and red tail are give-aways. Perches in a noticeably horizontal position. Sexes indistinguishable. A small introduced population near Perth.

Similar species: Initially could be confused with several other common finches found in towns, but those won't have the grey front and red mask.

Ecology: Occurs in a wide variety of treed habitats with a dense understorey, or shrubs and thickets where the birds spend most of their time. Moves through weedy areas and tall rank grasses in urban areas as well. Consumes many types of seeds taken while perched on the stems or the ground. Usually seen in flocks of 10–20. Call is a high-pitched *seet*.

Breeding: Nesting is vaguely communal, with pairs building their ball-shaped grass nests near each other.

Interactions with people: Rare.

DID YOU KNOW?

While still quite common, it is badly affected by the removal of thickets, including the invasive lantana shrub.

Nutmeg Mannikin

Lonchura punctulata
Family: Estrildidae: Finches and Mannikins

Introduced finch of disturbed, weedy areas along the eastern coast.

SIZE:

DISTRIBUTION:

HOME:

FOOD:

ACTIVE ZONE:

Identification: A dark-brown grass finch with a delicately scalloped front which is often difficult to make out unless in full sunlight. Usually remains well hidden within dense grasses or thickets, but sometimes ventures into the open to forage. Sexes identical.

Similar species: Most likely to be confused with the native Chestnut-breasted Mannikin, which can be found in the same habitat with tall grasses, but that species has bold chocolate, chestnut and white plumage.

Ecology: A native of South East Asia, where it occupies similar habitats as here: weedy edges of public parks and golf courses, cane fields and vacant lots. Consumes a wide variety of grass seeds. In Australia, usually seen in pairs or small flocks. Has a rather quiet *it-it-it* call.

Breeding: The pair build the nest together, an oversized ball of finely woven grasses with a side entrance, usually placed in the dense branches of a small tree.

Interactions with people: Although found mainly in urban landscapes, it tends not to interact with people.

DID YOU KNOW?

Originally brought to Australia as a cage bird. The numerous populations scattered along the eastern coast originate from aviary escapees.

House Sparrow

Passer domesticus
Family: Passeridae: Old World Sparrows

Until recently, the ultimate city denizen, scavenging crumbs beneath every café table.

M   F

SIZE:

DISTRIBUTION:

HOME:

FOOD:

ACTIVE ZONE:

Identification: The urban bird, familiar to the point of being virtually unnoticed. Small, boisterous finch; the male has a rich hazel back and wings and a splendid black bib while the female is duller and has no bib. Top of the head is grey. Its chirping is the soundtrack for towns and cities everywhere.

Similar species: Easily confused with the Eurasian Tree Sparrow, which has a black cheek spot and brown cap.

Ecology: One of the most abundant and widespread birds on the planet, having been taken around the world by European settlers. A generalist grain-eater, it pilfers grain fed to chickens and horses, and consumes weed seeds and human scraps. Gregarious and very tame, one of a few species now completely dependent on human settlements for survival.

Breeding: Breeds any time of the year though mostly in spring. Constructs large untidy nests of grass and fabric stuffed into the spaces behind eaves or roof cavities.

Interactions with people: Once the ubiquitous 'spag' or 'sparra' in every chicken coop, scavenging beneath the café tables downtown or nesting in the eaves. Still around, but much less common everywhere.

DID YOU KNOW?

Extraordinarily abundant for centuries, populations everywhere are now in dramatic decline. Possible reasons are fewer nesting spaces, less access to grain and a reduction in urban insect supplies.

Eurasian Tree Sparrow

Passer montanus
Family Passeridae: Old World Sparrows

More reserved cousin of the ubiquitous House Sparrow.

SIZE:

DISTRIBUTION:

HOME:

FOOD:

ACTIVE ZONE:

Identification: Typical 'sparra' with warm brown wings and back, grey-brown underparts and distinctive cheek patch. Unlike the House Sparrow, the sexes are identical.

Similar species: Very similar in habits to the House Sparrow, though seemingly less aggressive, so where they occur together, are usually less abundant or at least less visible. Often overlooked because it is so similar to the House Sparrow, so if you live in its distribution, it's always good to observe closely. Diagnostic features are the brown (instead of grey) cap and the prominent black cheek spot. The black bib is limited to the throat.

Ecology: Introduced, like the House Sparrow, to provide homesick Europeans with familiar sounds. Consumes seeds of almost any type and has prospered in regions where cereal grains are grown.

Breeding: Large, bulky grass nests are concealed in roof cavities and other structures.

Interactions with people: Closely tied to human settlements, stealing grain from chickens and nesting in eaves.

DID YOU KNOW?

Although found naturally throughout Europe and Asia, from Spain to Indonesia, the Australian birds almost certainly derive from United Kingdom stock.

European Goldfinch

Carduelis carduelis
Family: Fringillidae: Old World Finches

A gorgeous, melodic sprite, brightening many a garden and park.

SIZE:

DISTRIBUTION:

HOME:

FOOD:

ACTIVE ZONE:

Identification: Small and spirited. Distinctive head colours: vivid red face, with wide pure white stripe behind edges with black band. Stunning. Adding even more colour, the wings have consecutive strips of black, gold and black; unmistakable in flight. The sexes are almost identical (males have a bit more red on the head).

Similar species: Of the nine introduced finches in Australia none could be mistaken for the Goldie.

Ecology: A vibrant songster with a liquid call that tinkles through the air. A typical finch in its habits, consuming a wide variety of seeds and grains on the ground, but often perches on the seed heads of sturdy plants such as thistles and milkweed. Loves all sorts of modified places such as farms, parks and vacant blocks full of weeds.

Breeding: Pairs are rarely seen apart and form long-lasting bonds. The female builds the neat little grass cup nest alone, but the male helps with the raising of the young.

Interactions with people: Despite being introduced, these delightful sprites are mostly welcomed as pretty little birds with a lovely song. Become very confiding in the presence of people.

DID YOU KNOW?

They were brought to Australia as colourful cage birds to provide 'pleasant bird song', apparently because Australia didn't have birds with nice voices!

European Greenfinch

Chloris chloris
Family: Fringillidae: Old World Finches

A modest somewhat dull-looking finch with a buzzing song.

SIZE:

DISTRIBUTION:

HOME:

FOOD:

ACTIVE ZONE:

Identification: Plain olive-green with a minor flash of yellow in the wings in flight. Except in bright light, looks pretty drab. Emits a distinctive whirring buzz often from the tops of exposed perches. The sexes are almost identical (females are slightly duller).

Similar species: Can be mistaken for a House Sparrow when on the ground in the shade, but is distinctive in having no particularly distinctive features.

Ecology: A generalist grain and seed consumer, the European Greenfinch is found only in human-modified places such as plantations, farms and among groves of exotic trees. Almost never ventures into natural bushland, but can be seen in dune vegetation, near beaches.

Breeding: The female constructs a small, neat nest in a tree or tall shrub, often not very high above the ground. Both male and female feed the nestlings. Two or three breeding sessions each year.

Interactions with people: Far less confiding and conspicuous than the Goldfinch, but is a familiar bird in some parks and orchards.

DID YOU KNOW?
Although the adults only eat seeds and other plant materials, the chicks are fed on insects, mainly larvae, as are the chicks of most granivores.

NEXT
LEVEL BIRD
WATCHING

Black-faced Woodswallows
roosting in a row

HOW TO SEE MORE BIRDS IN YOUR BACKYARD

BIRDS NEED HABITAT; SOMEWHERE TO LIVE AND BREED SAFELY, WITH WATER, FOOD AND SHELTER.

Most of the birds featured in this book are tough and resilient; they aren't particularly fussy and can – and do – put up with a lot. But they do need space with some sort of suitable vegetation.

The problem with many new residential developments is that concrete and bitumen cover most of the ground not occupied by buildings. The only sizable areas with vegetation are overly manicured communal parklands or sports fields. These tend to have few trees and almost nothing in the way of understorey: shrubs and thickets.

So, let's think about the patch you do have some control over: your houseyard. Even if you don't have much space, you can do some things to encourage birds to visit. Think about this from the bird's point of view. There are three basic reasons why a bird may stop by at your place: water, food and shelter. Let's discuss each briefly.

Water

In the early 2020s, it seemed that a lack of water was the least of Australia's problems. Much of the eastern part of the continent was experiencing widespread flooding and the forecasts were predicting continuing wet.

On the positive side, vast areas that had been experiencing pronounced drought were flushed out, with floodwaters surging through barren landscapes and replenishing underground aquifers. In places like the Macquarie Marshes in central New South Wales and the vast Channel Country of south-west Queensland, many water birds (plus frogs and fish) had their best breeding seasons for decades. In places that had experienced the devastating bushfires of 2019–20, the deep soaking rain helped bring back life.

People tend to have very short memories. The reality is that large parts of this enormous continent are naturally very dry most of the time. The relentless sunshine and low humidity dry up

Eastern Spinebill in Pincushion Hakea

almost everything rapidly. This also happens in cities, although watering helps keep the lawns green and shrubs healthy. But that doesn't mean that it's easy to find a decent drink.

In other words, almost everyone should set up a bird bath or two. These can be out in the garden, on the verandah or attached to the balcony railings of your apartment. They need to be kept clean and checked for unwanted additions such as bones and desiccated food items placed there by crows and ravens (a remarkably common event), plus mozzies if the water is stagnant. A well-maintained bird bath can be one of the simplest ways to see more birds.

Food

Feeding wild birds is an astonishingly controversial topic in Australia – more so than in any other country on earth. The reasons for this are still unclear. Attracting them by offering food is pretty obvious, and enormous numbers of people do exactly that, despite the widespread opposition.

So, the question is: can we feed birds safely and sustainably? Let's look at several big statements. (For a lot more detail, see my earlier book, *Feeding the Birds at Your Table*.)

BIRDS DON'T NEED TO BE FED

Even though they may look ravenous and scoff every last morsel of whatever you offer, wild birds – even those living in cities – do not need any of the food we provide. I'll say that again: they don't need it! The exceptions are just that: exceptions. The local wildlife may benefit from some momentary provisioning following major natural catastrophes, such as prolonged drought, flood, cyclones or bushfires. But only until conditions improve. Otherwise, birds don't require our offerings. Even the individuals that visit bird feeders daily obtain almost all of their necessary nutrition from natural sources.

And thank goodness! Because no matter how careful we might be, human-provided foods can't offer everything wild animals need – and they can find the foods they need by themselves. Sure, they may enjoy the seeds, bread or mince placed out on the feeder. But these things are best thought of as a quick snack:

a cuppa and a bickie rather than a complete meal. That should be a great relief. It means that we aren't providing their daily dietary requirements; we can't! And that doesn't matter.

That's not welcome news to a lot of people. Plenty of folks feed 'their' birds regularly, firmly believing that the birds really need them. Indeed, many people feel if they stopped, their birds would suffer, starve or worse.

The reality is that the birds around us are not dependent on our provisions, no matter how carefully they are prepared or how expensive they are. In fact, they don't need any of it, though they will happily take advantage of the offerings. Instead of the birds being dependent, it turns out that it's the people who can't stop. Thankfully, they can (stop feeding) and the birds will hardly notice.

We think the feeders are for the birds. Actually, the feeders are for us. But the birds don't seem to mind. Our challenge is to feed them without harm.

FEEDING BIRDS CAN BE HARMFUL

I'm sure you're aware of the many reasons you should not feed birds:

- they may become dependent;
- feeding only benefits already common species;
- it increases aggressive interactions at feeders;
- it can attract vermin;
- it may lead to the spread of disease;
- and lots of others as well.

All of these are genuine concerns, but there's only limited evidence that most are of significance.

The one issue that is of incontrovertible importance, however, is the idea that bird feeders may facilitate the spread of diseases. It's easy to understand why. When we offer food in one small place where many birds come to feed – often with several species jostling for access – we have encouraged them to do something they would never do naturally. A flock of lorikeets foraging in a flowering tree or pigeons eating seeds on the ground is always spread out. Cramming together on a feeder, standing and defecating on the food, is just asking for trouble. If any of these birds is sick, spreading the infection is virtually inevitable.

As far as we know, Australia has been spared the catastrophic and deadly epidemics of bird diseases that have spread like wildfire through wild bird populations in the northern hemisphere. Just two of these, so-called House Finch Disease or Mycoplasmal conjunctivitis in the United States and a trichomoniasis infection in the United Kingdom, were responsible for reducing the populations of House Finches by 60 per cent and Greenfinches by 35 per cent in their respective countries. Those are terrifying figures. In both cases, the contagion was clearly due to, and spread by, bird feeders.

These tragic but avoidable occurrences have led to a serious re-think about the importance of keeping feeders clean at all times (though not to rethinking the feeding of birds in the first place). This point cannot be overstated: if you are going to feed birds, you must keep the feeder – whatever its design – scrupulously clean. That means careful scrubbing. *Every single day*.

TYPES OF FOODS

The next question – what should you provide as food – will come down to what types of birds you want to attract. In many cases, it will just be the birds already visiting! Whether these are birds already being fed further up your street or that they know a sucker when they see one, the situation is the same: they are expecting you to offer something.

Unless you are already feeding birds, my strong suggestion is not to start. Yes, those butcherbirds or Crimson Rosellas may appear hungry, but don't fall for it! Thay're probably visiting you because the folks from up the street are away and their feeder is empty. Let them forage for natural foods instead.

If you still want to feed, follow a few simple rules. (Please note that this does not apply to feeding birds in public places, like a picnic area or at the beach. In those places, don't! Especially if they are after bread or chips.)

AVOID HUMAN FOODS

Never offer anything made specifically for people: so bread, pastry, cake, chips, crisps, salami, sausage, cheese and mince are all no-nos. Among other things, these all have way too much sugar, fat and salt. If it was meant for people, it's almost certainly no good for birds. (I'm not going to comment on whether they are good for people either!)

Unfortunately, mince – the universal go-to for these types of birds, mainly because it's cheap and convenient – is a terrible bird food: it's sticky and contains far too little calcium. Both features can lead to serious problems for the birds.

OFFER APPROPRIATE SNACKS

If the birds are insectivores or carnivores (magpies, kookaburras, butcherbirds, etc), something meaty – with high protein – is required. Not mince, for reasons mentioned! The simplest alternative to mince is pet food which, while far from ideal, is at least formulated for animals. Thankfully, a number of products from specialist pet food shops are designed to replicate the nutrition found in insects.

If the birds are seed-eaters (granivore), plenty of good seed mixes are available at pet shops. Only purchase brands made by pet food companies. And avoid 'singles' (one type of seed), especially sunflowers (all parrots adore them, but they have far too much oil).

FEEDING BY PLANTING

But what about natural food rather than all these human-made products? Maybe we could place plants in our gardens that provide flowers and fruit for consuming? Choosing the best species can be tricky. Some seemingly simple decisions can have serious unintended consequences. The most significant of these has been the impact of all the nectar-bearing plants now found in almost every houseyard in the country.

Cultivars (variants bred specifically to emphasise certain features) of callistemons (bottlebrush) and grevilleas (spider-flowers), now have flowers dramatically enhanced in size and colour. Not only are they spectacular and enormous, they provide sugary goodness year-round, so Noisy Miners, and Rainbow Lorikeets especially, have exploded in numbers. In the last decade Rainbows have become the most abundant bird in every capital city and many other cities as well.

This might sound great – but the problem is that both miners and lorikeets are extremely aggressive and territorial, outcompeting almost all other rivals and utterly dominating bird communities. Noisy Miners are especially detrimental, driving away all smaller species (and plenty of larger ones). As many people now realise, if you have miners, you won't get much else. The presence of Noisy Miners is now officially recognised as a major threatening process, alongside habitat destruction and climate change. A smallish native honeyeater causing massive biodiversity loss? Aided and abetted simply by sticking a gorgeous 'Honey Gem' grevillea in the front garden? Apparently. This unsettling example shows how a seemingly benign decision can contribute to big and unwelcome changes to the bird communities we love.

Believe it or not, miners and all the so-called honeyeaters mostly eat insects; the nectar gives them a temporary sugar-rush, but they need protein and many other nutrients. In fact, the diets of the majority of birds that live in cities consist of mainly insects and other invertebrates (seed-eaters such as finches and parrots are the main exceptions). Apart from specialist worm and below-ground grub foragers like Magpies, almost all of these high-protein snacks are gleaned directly from the foliage of trees and shrubs.

This raises an obvious but unusual opportunity to assist some of the smaller insectivorous birds, the species often having the hardest time hanging out in town: planting shrubs that attract insects.

Generally, deliberately trying to bring plant-chewing bugs into your garden might not seem like the best idea. Don't most people want less insects? Probably, but if we want to attract some of the smaller birds, almost all of which are insectivorous, providing insect morsels is a logical start. This can be done simply by introducing various native shrubs to your yard. Yes, more plants, but this time, those that attract insects that attract birds. Simple.

Choosing the best insect-attracting plants will depend on many factors, but the general principle is to use species that occur locally. Such plants will be more suited to your soil type and climate and therefore more likely to flourish. Seek advice from local authorities such as plant nurseries or councils, and ask for their lists of recommended native plants.

Shelter

If you bring in more birds by providing food in the form of flowers and insects on native plants, you're already taking care of the third requirement: shelter. Those shrubs and small trees may also be places where smaller species can hide and rest. Or not. It depends on the structure of the plants themselves.

Grevilleas and banksias are often spindly and thin, not really offering anywhere for birds to hide. Others, like callistemons and hakeas, often have dense, complex branches and limbs, ideal for little birds to disappear away from predators, or from bird bullies. Miners, I'm talking about you.

While Noisy Miners are the worst, other large honeyeaters – wattlebirds, friarbirds and Blue-faced Honeyeaters – can be just as bad. The trick is providing places close to the ground for small birds to discreetly shelter. Dense, spiky shrubs and thickets allow these vulnerable smaller species to hide while the bullies carry on in the canopy above.

Numerous studies have shown that a dense shrub layer allows a range of smaller birds to successfully co-exist with despotic Noisy Miners. We will never be able to remove them, but it may be possible to alter the landscape so that the little guys have a fighting chance.

But, if you want to see more birds in your backyard, you also need to think about your neighbourhood.

FACING UP TO SOME BIG ISSUES

IT WILL BE NO SURPRISE TO THE READERS OF THIS BOOK THAT WE ARE CURRENTLY EXPERIENCING A GLOBAL BIODIVERSITY CRISIS.

This is partly associated with the effects of climate change, which is exacerbating all of the 'traditional' threats – loss of habitat, the impacts of invasive species, the spread of deadly diseases. We are learning the hard way how the clearing of land is leading to devastating floods, while storms and droughts increase in intensity.

The fact that everything in the natural world is interconnected in ways we barely understand is leading to diverse – and perverse – catastrophes wherever you look. For example, the ancient links between plant flowering, the insects that reproduce in response, and the timing of bird breeding activity to correspond with the maximum availability of insects for their nestlings, are critically important to each of the components. Yet, all over the world, these crucial links are becoming decoupled, with devastating impacts. Unless they are monitored carefully, it's easy to overlook them. These changes may be subtle or inconspicuous.

One symptom of climate change that is impossible to miss is the catastrophic bushfires turning entire ecosystems into nothing but charred carbon. Recent fires in Australia (and in many other countries) are among the most significant environmental tragedies. Our country alone saw a total of 24 million hectares destroyed, over 100 000 farm animals dead and possibly three billion native animals killed. The word used to describe the bushfire conditions at the time – catastrophic – can be accurately applied globally.

Unfortunately, yet another global environmental disruption is underway: urbanisation. This transformation of natural or rural landscapes into cities, or more accurately, sprawling suburbs – places designed exclusively for people – is usually rapid and total. Virtually nothing remains apart from some large trees in the fragments designated as green space. This process is accelerating around the world, and the overall impact on biodiversity is so great that it is now expected to be the primary cause of extinctions in the current century.

Laughing Kookaburra watching the scene below

It's hard to imagine why replacing a few trees with houses could be that significant. Well, it is, and here's why.

The places where people first choose to settle are almost always where there are fertile soil, a good water supply and good proximity to key resources – timber, clay, land for agriculture – needed to survive and establish a long-term foothold. Naturally, wildlife loves such places as well, for many of the same reasons. In other words, our cities are usually sited in biodiversity hot-spots. Understandably – and unfortunately – the areas where cities are located support more species of wildlife than other areas. This also means these areas have more rare and endangered creatures, with an increased likelihood of local populations disappearing altogether.

As the space occupied by towns expands, most species can persist only in the remnants of the original forests or woodland that remain. These patches support and represent the diversity of the original biota for the area in which they occur. As such, they are invaluable. Irreplaceable. Preserving them is of critical importance.

So, if you want to see more birds in your neighbourhood, ensuring that these places are safe is vital. Some may already be conservation reserves, but others may still be available for development. These patches must be protected.

So, a fair warning: becoming a better bird watcher is going to make you even more aware of the numerous environmental concerns we face. Learning that your local council plans to replace the patch of bush nearby with housing – or remove the ancient eucalypts with hollows currently occupied by rosellas, cockatoos, bats and gliders – will make you more likely to do something about it.

Landscape matters

Perhaps your interest in birds started by simply noticing them through the kitchen window, from the balcony or out in the garden. It doesn't matter where, but only a limited number of species can be seen in these places. Once you get the birdwatching bug, you'll want to see a lot more species. This will mean travelling further afield, perhaps the large park nearby or the conservation reserve in the next suburb. As you move around with your bird senses alert, you will begin to realise that the greatest diversity of species tends to be in places with the greatest variety of habitats.

The park across the street may include stands of trees, shrubs, perhaps a pond or two, all set in a wide expanse of well-mown lawn. Such places, limited in the variety of habitats available, will probably support some familiar birds. In contrast, a large patch of natural bushland, with extensive understorey, sections of grassland and large waterbodies, will almost certainly have a far greater variety of species. The point is that to see a lot of different species, you need to visit places with a variety of habitats.

Begin to picture the layout of the good birding locations, how these are arranged over the area, how far apart they are. This is taking a 'landscape-level' view of the area, taking note of the relationships between the remnants, parks, waterbodies or any other relevant places. You can do this easily by looking at these places on your phone or laptop.

Why not try this now? Open the map app and change the view type to 'satellite' to show a photographic representation of the landscape. Now look for places with lots of tree cover; these are almost always the best spots for finding birds. Are these part of a large reserve, or are they an island of green surrounded by the 'urban matrix' (a sprawl of mostly residential areas)? If they are isolated, how far are they from the nearest natural area?

The way these places are arranged is important because isolated patches of habitat, located far from similar patches are particularly vulnerable to local extinction. A serious bushfire, a severe flood, a prolonged drought, an epidemic of a severe disease or the destruction of habitat can threaten the very existence of the animals (and plants) that live in these places.

Such phenomena can occur at any time. Some big disruptions such as bushfires may even be essential for the germination of certain seeds. Sometimes, even if the event wipes out a species, it may be replaced naturally from existing populations in the vicinity.

However, if the patch is isolated and far from the next area of similar habitat, and is surrounded by a hostile matrix such as suburbs, the likelihood of natural recolonisation becomes increasingly low.

And, while nearly all birds can fly, we now realise that many small forest-dwelling species never cross open space of any significant width. Studies have shown that even 45 metres is too far for some. These are the birds most threatened by urbanisation, especially the fragmentation associated with the expanding road network. Fairy-wrens, robins, scrub-wrens and small honeyeaters, for example, are particularly reticent about being exposed when crossing open areas, presumably because they are sensibly concerned about predators.

Of course, most birds don't have such qualms and regularly fly over open spaces. Many species that live mainly within the foliage or dense understorey fly between these places. Even so, they tend to 'island hop' using whatever small clumps of trees that remain as stepping stones and are reluctant to fly too far if completely exposed. Having suitable habitat at regular intervals can make a big difference to their ability and willingness to travel through the landscape.

The remnants of natural bushland and isolated patches that exist in your neighbourhood are critically important. How they are positioned, and the distances between them, matters. As you get to know the various places birds are using to traverse the area, you will become aware of the likely safe routes and way-stations dotted around. And one of those way-stations might just be your garden.

Taking a 'landscape' perspective is really an attempt to see the area in which you live the way the birds do. And it's quite likely other people in your neighbourhood will be thinking along the same lines. Getting to know the birds in your neighbourhood is even better when sharing your information with people around you. I encourage you to band together to take action, or organise a group to meet with the local council; such connections can make a big difference.

New Holland Honeyeater
on the move

CAN BIRD WATCHING MAKE YOU HAPPY?

CAN BIRD WATCHING MAKE YOU HAPPY?

That may sound like a silly question. Of course it can, or at least it will keep you happily occupied for a while. You may even become excited, enthusiastic or grateful for witnessing an unusual behaviour, or seeing a special bird. And you may even encounter times of boredom, frustration and anger. No new species for a month! Kids disturbing the birds! Dogs running free on the beach where birds are breeding! GAH!

Emotions – positive and negative – are definitely part of the experience. But there is more to this pastime than feeling temporarily good. Because birds live outside, seeing them means getting out of the house and into the open air. You will also need to walk, listen, watch carefully, be attentive. Your senses will be activated and your mind will become alert. All of these things are good for you.

But one of the realities of modern life is that our urban landscapes seem to leave little room for nature. And the possibility of any sort of interaction with nature in any meaningful way seems remote. This 'extinction of experience' – loss of connection with the natural world – makes it seem as though 'nature' is in some other, distant location.

Thankfully, and self-evidently, no matter how built-up your neighbourhood is, all you need to do is stick your head out the front door and listen. In no time you'll hear the screech of lorikeets, the cawing of a crow (or raven) or the chatter of honeyeaters (probably miners) in the street trees. Almost everywhere in cities and towns throughout the country there are plenty of birds.

But a far more significant element to this story is our need to spend time out in natural settings to be fully healthy and happy. Even the simplest interactions with nature – being able to see trees, look at flowers, see water running in a creek, hear birdsong – have benefits for mental health and physical wellbeing.

An immense body of serious research has demonstrated that some form of connection with nature is extremely important for everyone. And you don't need to meditate in the rainforest; just

Female Superb Fairy-wren in full song

being able to walk through a park with trees and gardens can decrease levels of depression and lead to more rapid healing of injuries. Hospital patients who have a view of real trees spend significantly less time in bed than those who only have pictures of trees in their rooms.

In one of the most remarkable studies of all, people recovering from serious brain injuries recovered far more quickly if they were able to walk through a wooded parkland rather than city streets. Simply by walking among the trees!

Equally astonishing – and important – is the discovery of a 'dose' aspect to connecting with nature. Like medicine, the higher to dose, the stronger the effect. But without the worry of overdosing!

The studies investigating these aspects of 'nature for healing' have found some characteristics of natural sounroundings are more effective: the greater the variety and complexity, the better. From the perspective of healing and wellbeing, it doesn't matter whether you know much about what you are experiencing. The natural elements – not made by humans – make the difference.

We somehow know nature should be complicated and messy. Strangely, this can be just what complicated and messy lives might need. In many of these studies, 'engaging with nature' was simply wandering through an urban park. So, if walking passively among the trees can help, what about birds?

Great question! Watching birds is most definitely not a passive pastime. You have to be watchful and attentive, scanning the foliage for the slightest movement, ears open for calls, staying still, then moving quickly but silently, straining the senses, trying desperately to detect a fleeting flutterer. It's anything but passive with senses, body and emotions all interacting and switched on. And that's what makes the difference.

Bird watching is a recognised practice for treating depression and anxiety. But you don't have to suffer such problems to benefit. Research from the United Kingdom has demonstrated that people who regularly watched birds in their gardens felt significantly more relaxed and connected to nature than those who didn't.

Studies were also able to point out that a major reason for the well-established 'green space' effect was probably the presence of birds (and their song) in the trees.

So, it seems, bird watching *can* make you happy. Even if you were very unhappy to begin with. And the birds themselves don't even have a clue. We need them, maybe even more than they need us.

Sulphur-crested Cockatoos can be very affectionate

WHERE TO NEXT?

BIRDING CAN BE ADDICTIVE,
IN A GOOD WAY!

Becoming 'addicted' might even be the first step in becoming more aware of birds and their habitats, in being curious about their lives and wanting to ensure that they have safe environments in which to thrive. You see, learning how to identify the birds in your neighbourhood is just the beginning. In fact, we would be delighted to hear that you no longer need this book and have started to use one of the 'serious' field guides with confidence.

Once you have become adept at IDing and have become reasonably interested in your birds, it might be time to contribute to the critically important process of gathering information on Australia's birds. You may think that is far-fetched or ridiculously ambitious for someone without a scientific background. Actually, even the simplest lists of local birds can be of genuine value, especially when combined with all the other information provided by lots of bird watchers, just like you.

If all the records from people like you could be gathered together, it might be possible to answer questions that no single researcher could ever possibly hope to do. In what has become known as 'Citizen Science', one of the first projects Cornell Lab of Ornithology in New York tried was to invite ordinary bird watchers to send in their basic personal records. This started simply, and the lab slowly developed easy-to-follow instructions that ensured the data being gathered could be trusted and reliable.

Since those early days, Citizen Science has covered an extraordinary range of topics and species, though none greater than the development of eBird, also developed by the Cornell Lab, and now just over 20 years old. Since it began, about 820 000 people have sent in more than 1.3 billion bird observations globally. This truly monumental data set is available to anyone who wants to use it, completely transforming understanding of things like migration, distributions and breeding cycles.

And you can be part of this extraordinary program, no matter how insignificant you may think your birds are. Simply visit the eBird website (ebird.org/home), download the app and you're on your way!

Little Pied Cormorants resting after fishing

In Australia, you'll find BirdLife Australia's similar program, *Birdata* (birdata.birdlife.org.au), and other platforms such as *iNaturalist* (www.inaturalist.org) and the *Atlas of Living Australia* (www.ala.org.au), which function in a similar way – but include wildlife beyond birds. All have smart-phone apps designed to be easy to use in the field.

However, the website most relevant to the objectives of this book is *Birds In Backyards*, a wonderful and important endeavour run by BirdLife Australia. Visit the BIBY website (www. birdsinbackyards.net) and check out the comprehensive information available.

As well as an excellent and intuitive identification guide (Bird Finder), there is lots of practical information on how to change your backyard into habitat birds will love (Creating Places) and instructions on how to participate in regular seasonal bird surveys. One of the most exciting aspects of being involved in this program is seeing how the information you collect compares to other places across the country.

REFERENCES AND USEFUL RESOURCES

Anon. 2021. Can birdwatching really improve your mental health? The science says yes. <www.birdlife.org/news/2021/10/05/can-birdwatching-really-improve-our-mental-health-the-science-says-yes>.

Abbott, I. 2009. Aboriginal names of bird species in south-west Western Australian, with suggestions for their adoption into common usage. *Conservation Science Western Australia*, 7, pp 213–278.

Black, A, McEntee, J, Sutton, P and Breen, G. 2018. The pre-European distribution of the Galah, *Eolophus roseicapilla* Vieillot: Reconciling scientific, historical and ethno-linguistic evidence. *South Australian Ornithologist*, 42, pp 37–57.

Clarke, PA. 2023. *Aboriginal Peoples and Birds in Australia: Historical and cultural relationships*. CSIRO Publishing, Melbourne.

Fuller, RA, Irvine, KN, Devine-Wright, P, Warren, PH and Gaston, KJ. 2007. Psychological benefits of greenspace increase with biodiversity. *Biology Letters*, 3, pp 390–494.

Fuller, RA and Irvine, KN. 2010. Interactions between people and nature in urban environments. In *Urban Ecology*. KJ Gaston (ed), Cambridge University Press, Cambridge, pp 134–171.

Hammoud, R, Tognin, S, Burgess, L, Bergou, N, Smythe, M, Gibbons, J, Davidson, N, Afifi, A, Bakolis, I and Mechelli, A. 2022. Smartphone-based ecological momentary assessment reveals mental health benefits of birdlife. *Scientific Reports*, 12: 17589.

Jones, DN. 2019. *Feeding the Birds at Your Table: A guide for Australia*. NewSouth Publishing, Sydney.

Menkhorst, P, Rogers, D, Clarke, R, Davies, J, Marsack, P and Franklin, K. 2017. *The Australian Bird Guide*. CSIRO Publishing, Melbourne.

Miller, JR. 2005. Biodiversity conservation and the extinction of experience. *Trends in Ecology & Evolution*, 20, pp 430–434.

Pyle, RM. 2003. Nature matrix: Reconnecting people and nature. *Oryx*, 37, pp 206–214.

Sadokierski, Z, Burrell, A, Hochuli, D, Martin, J and van Dooran, T. 2022. *A Guide to the Creatures in Your Neighbourhood*. Murdoch Books, Perth.

Field guides

It might seem strange to say it, but we want you to outgrow this book as quickly as possible. It is intended to provide some crucial first steps, but sooner or later, you will need more information.

Bird watchers in Australia are spoiled for choice when it comes to field guides. By far the most authoritative and detailed is *The Australian Bird Guide* (even better, a more compact version was published in 2022, *The Compact Australian Bird Guide: Concise Edition*). The arrangement of the species used in the book you are holding, as well as a lot of information, was adapted from this brilliant tome.

Websites

Many websites can help you identify birds and provide an abundance of additional information. These are the most useful.

Birds in Backyards [birdsinbackyards.net]
Hosted by BirdLife Australia, BIBY is literally the closest thing to an online version of this book, but with a lot more details. Not only will you find easy-to-follow tips on identification and fascinating information about bird behaviour, entire sections are devoted to transforming your garden into a haven for birds. You'll learn what plants to choose or avoid and even read a sensible discussion about the vexed question: is feeding birds a good idea?

eBird Australia [ebird.org/australia]
Developed by the Cornell Lab of Ornithology, eBird in the largest and most detailed source of information about birds in the world. As well as being extremely easy to use and follow, it guides you gently towards a confident identification. Importantly, eBird includes plenty of recorded bird calls, which can make a very big difference in confident identification.

Apps
Apps are mainly online versions of field guides, but with additional bells and whistles, including calls. Merlin is the IDing companion to eBird and as both come from Cornell Lab of Ornithology, you know they are the gold standard. They have

recently developed an Australia-specific module. The final two apps are designed specifically for matching photographs to their massive databases and letting the AI do the ID. Still a new technology (as an app, that is) but, given the nature of machine learning, it will get better over time.

Morcombe's Birds of Australia (mydigitalearth.com)

Pizzey & Knight Birds of Australia (Gibbon Multimedia)

Merlin Bird ID (Cornell Lab)

Australian Bird Identification (NatureAi)

Smart Bird ID Australia (Yellow Cardinal)

Website URLs throughout this book were all correct as at 2 June 2023.

Little Wattlebird foraging
in callistemon

ACKNOWLEDGMENTS

The original idea for this book came from a genuine beginner bird watcher, Emma Hutchinson, who discovered her local birds during those strange COVID lock-down times, fell in love with them and wanted to get to know them well. Emma represents the very people the book was designed for: someone who wants to know what their local birds are called, and learn a bit more about them. Not only is she a keen novice birdo, she actually works at NewSouth Publishing, which was rather handy. This is the third book we have completed together, but never this closely. Her support for the project, her personal insights, endless enthusiasm and ideas – and occasional cattle-prod – kept this project moving forward. She also selected and arranged all the wonderful images.

This book was very much a team effort. As well as Emma's oversight at NewSouth, Madeleine Kane undertook the daunting design role, where key changes were suggested throughout the development of the book. I am forever indebted to super-editor Jessica Perini who found herself editing under extreme pressure – I really appreciate your efforts, Jess. When things got serious at the very end, two calm and professional people stepped up, bringing everything together: Josephine Pajor-Markus as typesetter and extraordinary proofreader Anne Savage. Their patience and attention to detail was exceptional.

When the type and aim of the book began to take shape, I knew I was going to need plenty of help and advice. Thankfully, I already knew who to talk to. Holly Parsons and Monica Awasthy have been involved with Birds in Backyards (BIBY), the urban birds flagship of BirdLife Australia, for many years, and were crucial in helping make the difficult decisions about what needed to be included and what didn't. Settling on (only) 139 species was always going to be contentious, but we worked it out in the end. And we are still talking!

The legendary Sean Dooley was involved from the very first inklings of this project and ever-present along the way. In many ways, Sean should have been a full co-author but it wasn't to be. Instead, he's played a cameo role, generously sharing his knowledge right through to the end.

We always knew that First Nations input was crucial. At the very beginning, Robyn Horwell made a major contribution in compiling a huge catalogue of Indigenous bird names in consultation with elders from the Wiradjuri community, one of the largest tribal regions in Australia. This is my home territory, around Wagga Wagga in central New South Wales, where much of the writing was completed. I am grateful to Sue Bazzana, who negotiated a quiet writing space in St Martin's Residential College at Charles Sturt University and Louise Freckelton and David Bray of Highfield, a spectacular property in the lower Snowy Mountains region. Their incredible (and totally offline) cottage, Kestrel Nest, could hardly be a more ideal writer's retreat (check it out: www.highfieldfarmwoodland.com/kestrel-nest-ecohut).

Our understanding of Indigenous relationships with birds changed dramatically through two crucial individuals. Philip Clarke's landmark volume, *Aboriginal Peoples and Birds in Australia*, was published just in time for us, and proved to be a profound and humbling resource. Many of the First Nations details we have included here came from Philip's extraordinarily rich material, collated from all over the continent, and through direct discussions with First Nations peoples on Country. Philip was a kind and patient correspondent as well.

I met Coen Hird through a panel we served on at the 2023 Brisbane Writers Festival. Coen is a young research scientist at the University of Queensland and proud trawlwoolway man from the lutruwita (Tasmanian) community. The conversations I had with Coen fundamentally changed my naïve and simplistic assumptions about Indigenous concepts of wildlife and their relationships with certain species. I remain forever grateful for his patience and invaluable insights. In addition, Lea Gardam, from the South Australian Museum, provided valuable input.

As always, I owe everything to my partner Liz, who listened to too many conversations about birds she had never heard of, as well as putting up good naturedly with her so-called house-husband's continual absences, far too often.

Picture credits

Shutterstock images

ii Rainbow Lorikeet, On the Wing Photography

vi-vii White-faced Heron, Matt Sheumack

viii Male Scarlet Honeyeater, Peter6172

4–5 Noisy Miners, Henry Rombe

6 Olive-backed Sunbirds, through sam eyes

12 Pied Butcherbirds, alybaba

21 Willy Wagtail, alybaba

24–25 Australian Pelicans, Jodie Nash

26 Australian Pelican, sirtravelalot

27 Great Cormorant, Bouke Atema

28 Little Black Cormorant, Imogen Warren

29 Little Pied Cormorant, Mandy Creighton

30 Australian Darter, Nicolette Coombs

31 Silver Gull, Chris Cousins

32 Bush Stone-curlew, Ken Griffiths

33 Masked Lapwing, Viktor Hejna

34 Black Swan, Martin Fowler

34 Black Swans, yougoigo

36 Australian Wood Ducks, Wright Out There

37 Grey Teal, Imogen Warren

38 Pacific Black Duck, Alex Cooper Photography

39 Northern Mallards, tomashko

40 Australasian Grebe, Ken Griffiths

41 White-faced Heron, Tessa Palmer

42 Male Great Egret, Andreas Ruhz

43 Great Egret, Rejean Aline Bedard

44 Intermediate Egret, Ken Griffiths

45 Eastern Cattle Egret, Photodigitaal.nl

46 Little Egret, David Havel

47 Eastern Reef Egret, Paulose NK

48 Australian White Ibis, Avril Morgan

49 Straw-necked Ibis, Robert Cerny

50 Australasian Swamphen, Ron Kolet

51 Eurasian Coot, MiQ

52–53 Eurasian Coots, Simonas Minkevicius

54 Dusky Moorhen, Ken Griffiths

55 Australian Brush-turkey, Belle Ciezak

56 Orange-footed Scrubfowl, Agami Photo Agency

57 Eastern Osprey, Alex Cooper Photography

58 White-bellied Sea-Eagle, Barry Callister

59 Whistling Kite, Russ Jenkins

60 Brahminy Kite, Imogen Warren

61 Brahminy Kite, Pete Evans

62 Black Kite, Imogen Warren

63 Brown Goshawk, Russ Jenkins

64 Pacific Baza, Belle Ciezak

65 Nankeen Kestrel, Stephanie Owen

66 Australian Hobby, Imogen Warren

67 Peregrine Falcon, Sriram Bird Photographer

69 Eastern Barn Owl, Imogen Warren

70 Southern Boobook, PomInPerth

71 Powerful Owl, Ken Griffiths

72 Tawny Frogmouth, David Steele

73 Yellow-tailed Black-Cockatoo, sompreaw

74 Gang-gang Cockatoo, Dirk Kotze

75 Galah, Alex Cooper Photography

76 Galahs, John Carnemolla

78 Long-billed Corella, Steven Giles

79 Western Corella, Serge Goujon

Even Australian Brush-turkeys spend time preening to look their best

INDEX

UNSW Press acknowledges the Bedegal people, the Traditional Owners of the unceded territory on which the Randwick and Kensington campuses of UNSW are situated, and recognises their continuing connection to Country and culture. We pay our respects to their Elders past and present.

A NewSouth book

Published by
NewSouth Publishing
University of New South Wales Press Ltd
University of New South Wales
Sydney NSW 2052
AUSTRALIA
https://unsw.press/

© Darryl Jones 2023
First published 2023

10 9 8 7 6 5 4 3 2

 A catalogue record for this book is available from the National Library of Australia

ISBN   9781742238050 (paperback)
            9781742239767 (ePDF)

Concept and development Emma Hutchinson
Design Madeleine Kane
Typesetting Josephine Pajor-Markus
Front cover image Male Gang-gang Cockatoo, David C Simon (Shutterstock)
Back cover image Tawny Frogmouths, Matt Sheumack (Shutterstock)
Back endpaper image Common Starlings, mutan (Shutterstock)
Printer Everbest

This book is printed on paper using fibre supplied from plantation or sustainably managed forests.